MW00470975

The Ave Guide to

Eucharistic
Adoration

"This guide does a great job of using the foundation of the Mass to draw us into deeper prayer through the gift of Adoration. The four themes drawn from the Mass help to remove any intimidation when approaching the altar for Adoration and lay out a clear plan without robbing the adorer of the space to receive grace, which is often a result of a hyperfocus on rubrics and schedules. This is an indispensable guide for making the most of your time in Adoration."

Rachel Bulman
Contributor to Word on Fire Catholic Ministries

"Filled with devotions and prompts for prayer, this essential guide to making a holy hour also presents a helpful history of how Eucharistic Adoration developed in the life of the Church. This resource for diving deeper into 'the Source and Summit' of our faith shouldn't be missed!"

Jackie and Bobby Angel
Catholic speakers, authors, and YouTubers

"*The Ave Guide to Eucharistic Adoration* provides a catechetical and inspirational resource for all Catholics. Rooted in the long-standing tradition of our faith and the writings of the saints, this book will prove a valuable point of reflection and prayer for Christian discipleship as we seek to follow the example of Mary of Bethany by sitting at the feet of Jesus in the Most Holy Eucharist."

Fr. Blake Britton
Author of *Reclaiming Vatican II*

"When one first begins to adore the Eucharist, one is faced with a terrifying fear. You have nothing to do but be alone before the Lord. Of course, that's the point. But it often takes a bit of time to simply rejoice in the Presence of the Beloved. *The Ave Guide to Eucharistic Adoration* is not an apologetics for the adoration of the Blessed Sacrament. Rather, it is intended—in short segments—to exercise men and women to adore the Eucharistic Lord. This resource will form the faithful to desire to dwell with the Eucharistic Lord."

Timothy P. O'Malley
Author of *Becoming Eucharistic People*

The Ave Guide to
Eucharistic Adoration

Ave Maria Press AVE Notre Dame, Indiana

Nihil Obstat: Reverend Monsignor Michael Heintz, PhD
            Censor Librorum

Imprimatur: Most Reverend Kevin C. Rhoades
            Bishop of Fort Wayne–South Bend
            Given at: Fort Wayne, Indiana, on 10 January 2023

The *Nihil Obstat* and *Imprimatur* are official declarations that a book or pamphlet is free of doctrinal or moral error. No implication is contained therein that those who have granted the *Nihil Obstat* or *Imprimatur* agree with its contents, opinions, or statements expressed.

Scripture texts in the "Sacred Writings and Sacred Readings" sections are taken from the *New American Bible, revised edition* © 2010, 1991, 1986, 1970 Confraternity of Christian Doctrine, Washington, DC, and are used by permission of the copyright owner. All Rights Reserved. No part of the *New American Bible* may be reproduced in any form without permission in writing from the copyright owner.

English translation of the *Catechism of the Catholic Church* for the United States of America copyright © 1994, United States Catholic Conference, Inc.—Libreria Editrice Vaticana. Used with permission.

Writer
Michael Amodei

Founded in 1865, Ave Maria Press is a ministry of the United States Province of Holy Cross.

www.avemariapress.com

Hardcover: ISBN-13 978-1-64680-220-3

E-book: ISBN-13 978-1-64680-221-0

Cover design by Christopher D. Tobin.

Text design by Kristen Hornyak Bonelli.

Printed and bound in the United States of America.

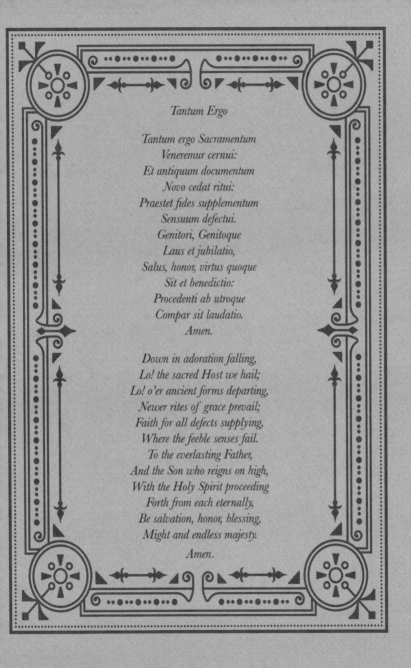

Tantum Ergo

Tantum ergo Sacramentum
Veneremur cernui:
Et antiquum documentum
Novo cedat ritui:
Praestet fides supplementum
Sensuum defectui.
Genitori, Genitoque
Laus et jubilatio,
Salus, honor, virtus quoque
Sit et benedictio:
Procedenti ab utroque
Compar sit laudatio.
Amen.

Down in adoration falling,
Lo! the sacred Host we hail;
Lo! o'er ancient forms departing,
Newer rites of grace prevail;
Faith for all defects supplying,
Where the feeble senses fail.
To the everlasting Father,
And the Son who reigns on high,
With the Holy Spirit proceeding
Forth from each eternally,
Be salvation, honor, blessing,
Might and endless majesty.
Amen.

Contents

Introduction

Watch and Pray

What comes to mind when you think about spending an hour alone before the Blessed Sacrament?

- "What would I do?"

- "Good idea, but with my schedule I just don't have the time."

- "I might fall asleep."

Let's focus a bit on that last thought. A church is a quiet place. Likely it would be darkened and nearly empty when you are there to pray. You could fall asleep. You wouldn't be the first!

In the Garden of Gethsemane on the night before Jesus's Passion and Death, he "advanced a little" from the apostles to pray on his own. When he returned, he did find all of them asleep. Jesus said to Peter, "Simon, are you asleep? Could you not keep watch for one hour? Watch and pray that you may not undergo the test. The spirit is willing but the flesh is weak" (Mk 14:37–38). Don't think of Jesus's words as condemning. Think of Jesus's words as hopeful. He told Peter to try again. "Watch and pray" are commands in the present or future tenses. These words are Jesus's indication to Peter that there would be another chance to spend an hour with him in prayer.

We have the same opportunity to spend an hour with Jesus before the Blessed Sacrament. If we "fail" the first time by being distracted, or giving up in less than sixty minutes, or falling asleep, he asks us, too, to try again. The benefits are tremendous! An hour before the Blessed Sacrament is a chance to overcome our other concerns, such as worldly issues—including the demands of a busy schedule—under the care of our Lord.

The long-held Catholic practice of spending an hour in Eucharistic Adoration before the Blessed Sacrament is known as a "holy hour." The main purpose of a holy hour is to be with Jesus and to look at him adoringly and lovingly while he looks at you in the same way. Interestingly, the Church doesn't offer a standard formula or set of prayers for what you should do when making a holy hour. Catholics do many different things other than sit in silence. They make prayers of penance. They offer thanksgiving for blessings. They pray for others. Some pray the Rosary or read scripture. And many people do indeed spend the entire hour in complete silence, letting God speak to them as they listen.

The History of Eucharistic Adoration

An appreciation and sense of awe in the Real Presence of Christ in the Eucharist has led to various teachings, practices, and devotions since the time of the apostles. There have been formal and communal elements of Eucharistic Adoration, such as the Forty-Hours Devotion, Perpetual Adoration, and Benediction. There have been Eucharistic congresses and Eucharistic processions. All of these practices include time for individual Eucharistic Adoration, though they are mostly communal in nature.

This book focuses on what you do in an individual holy hour, not in a particularly communal devotion like Benediction. Nevertheless, it is a worthy endeavor to be familiar with this history of Eucharistic Adoration in the Church—both communal practices and individual practices—before you begin. Listed below is a brief timeline of important events:

- St. Paul was forceful in reminding the community in Corinth that at their gathering for a communal meal—known by the Greek term for unconditional love, *agape*—the presence of the Eucharist must be treated differently and more reverently than ordinary food; it was, in fact, the Body and Blood of Christ. He then quoted for them words Jesus spoke at the first Eucharist at the Last Supper: This is my Body . . . This is my Blood. The text in 1 Corinthians 11:23–25 is the earliest written account of the institution of the Eucharist.

- In the third century, hermits, or monks, were allowed to keep the consecrated hosts in their caves or cells. The intention was so that the hermits could give themselves Holy Communion. But they also understood the spiritual grace of having the Real Presence of Jesus with them. They would also carry a particle of the host with them when they worked in the fields or traveled from one place to another. This practice was approved by the Church and known as *fermentum*, meaning "in an active state."

- Sometime after the Council of Nicaea in 325, the Eucharist began to be reserved in a special place in monasteries, convents, and churches. St. Basil, an Eastern bishop of the fourth century, is said to have divided the Eucharist into three parts after celebrating Mass. One part he consumed, the second part he gave to the monks, and the third part he placed in a tabernacle over the altar.

- A heretical statement by a French archdeacon, Berengarius, in the eleventh century, discounting Christ's Real Presence in the Eucharist, led to Pope St. Gregory VII writing a statement that said, in part, "that after the consecration they are the true body of Christ . . . and the true blood of Christ—which flowed from His side—and not just as a sign and by reason of the power of the sacrament, but in the very truth and reality of their substance and in what is proper to their nature" (quoted in *Mysterium Fidei*, 52). Pope Gregory's statement awakened in the Church great devotion to Christ in the Blessed Sacrament. St. Francis of Assisi was instrumental in leading a Eucharistic renaissance in the Church, fueled by his own personal devotion.

- In 1264, Pope Urban IV instituted the Feast of Corpus Christi, also known as the Solemnity of the Body and Blood of Jesus Christ. The pope reminded the Church that Jesus said before his Ascension that he would be with us always, even to the end of the world. Pope Urban emphasized that the truth of Jesus's statement is concretized in his bodily presence reserved in the Blessed Sacrament. Pope Urban commissioned St. Thomas Aquinas to write three hymns for the Feast of Corpus Christi, which was to be celebrated on the Thursday following Trinity Sunday. The hymns—"O Salutaris Hostia," "Tantum Ergo Sacramentum," and "Panis Angelicus"—remain part of the Church's Divine Office today.

- When the sanctifying Real Presence of Christ was questioned by the Protestant Reformers, the Council of Trent issued a declaration that "the only Son of God is to be adored in the Holy Sacrament of the Eucharist with the worship of latria [adoration], including external worship [outside of Mass]." The Council also encouraged processions and celebrations in featuring the presence of the Blessed Sacrament.

- In 1673, Jesus appeared to St. Margaret Mary Alacoque and shared the spiritual benefits of making a holy hour. He said making a holy hour would help to make atonement for the indifference that the world showed to his love for them. He asked her to make a holy hour between Thursday and Friday, recalling the night he prayed alone in the Garden of Gethsemane. In 1886, Pope Leo XIII issued an apostolic letter allowing the faithful to make a holy hour any day of the week. With proper preparations and conditions, Pope Leo offered the possibility for a plenary indulgence to be received for those spending one hour in Eucharistic Adoration.

- The Forty-Hours Devotion began in the late sixteenth century. The devotion consisted of forty hours of continual prayer before the Blessed Sacrament. It was guaranteed that at least one person would sit before the Blessed Sacrament during the entire devotion.

- Perpetual Adoration has been a practice in the Church since the fourth century when converts were asked to adore the exposed Blessed Sacrament for eight days before their Baptism. After the Council of Trent, Perpetual Adoration became the practice of several religious communities and institutes devoted to the practice.

- Benediction began in the thirteenth century. It is a communal occasion of readings, prayers, and songs to accompany the Blessed Sacrament being exposed on the altar in a monstrance or ciborium.

- A Eucharistic congress—that is, an event for gathering around the Eucharist by priests, religious, and laity—has taken place, often on an international basis, since it was proposed by a French laywoman, Marie-Marthe-Baptistine Tamisier, in the late nineteenth century. She promoted pilgrimages to places where Eucharistic miracles had taken place. The first international Eucharistic congress was held at Lille, France, in 1881.

- Since at least the fourteenth century, individual visits to the Blessed Sacrament have been a standard part of personal and communal prayer. According to canon law, "The church in which the Most Holy Eucharist is reserved is to be open to the faithful for at least some hours every day so that they can pray before the Most Blessed Sacrament" (937). Most Catholic churches are open for at least some hours each day for that purpose.

There is only one Sacrament of the Holy Eucharist, the Mass. Yet this one sacrament, summarized by

St. John Paul II in his first encyclical, *Redemptor Hominis*, confers grace on us in three different ways. "It is at one and the same time a Sacrifice-Sacrament, a Communion-Sacrament, and a Presence-Sacrament" (IV, 20). As a sacrifice, the Eucharist is a source of grace in which we are given the gift of repentance and the pardon of our sins. As a communion, we are nourished in receiving his Body and Blood, and we are also sustained in avoiding mortal sin. In Christ's Real Presence, we are given the opportunity to experience concretely the humanity of Christ, who is our salvation.

The Blessed Sacrament is the very source of the graces given by Christ, who once died for our sins and now through his Real Presence dispenses those graces to us who spend time in Eucharistic Adoration.

Eucharistic Adoration Is an Extension of Mass

This book offers several options for making a holy hour based on the Order of Mass.

Why the Mass? The first occasion of Eucharistic Adoration is at Mass when the priest holds up the consecrated host before Communion and says, "Behold, the Lamb of God, behold him who takes away the sins of the world." And yet our time to adore Christ in that moment is too short in duration. Over the centuries, Catholics have discovered that in order to really savor the immensity of the sacrifice performed and the love offered on our behalf at Mass, more time and effort are needed. Hence, in various forms through the centuries, the Church has welcomed the practice of Eucharistic Adoration—not as separate from the Mass, but as an extension of the Mass.

The Mass is itself divided into four parts:

- Introductory Rites
- Liturgy of the Word
- Liturgy of the Eucharist
- Concluding Rites

Each of these parts of the Mass has important elements worthy of deeper reflection and in consideration for further action. There is no better time and place to do that than before the Lord in the Blessed Sacrament.

Adoration and Penance

After the entrance and greeting, a Penitential Act takes place as part of the Introductory Rites. The *Didache*, a key first-century Church document, reveals that Christians began the Eucharist "after having confessed [their] transgressions, that [their] sacrifice may be pure" (14). Before the Second Vatican Council, the priest expressed penance *on behalf* of the gathered community. He recited prayers that spoke of his unworthiness to preside at the sacrifice of the Mass. Since the Second Vatican Council, there are many options for the faithful themselves to recall their sins and pause for reflection. Each of these particular rites concludes with the priest offering a prayer of absolution: "May almighty God have mercy on us, forgive us our sins, and bring us to everlasting life."

Anytime we are in the presence of the Lord, it is wise to examine our conscience, reflect on our failings, ask God's forgiveness, and accept his mercy.

Adoration and Word

Together with the Liturgy of the Eucharist, the Liturgy of the Word forms the central portion of the Mass. The Liturgy of the Word includes "the writings of the prophets"—that is, the Old Testament—and "the memoirs of the apostles" (their letters and the gospels) as named in the *Catechism of the Catholic Church* (1349) , which quotes from St. Justin Martyr's *First Apology*. From the earliest celebrations of the Mass, Christians shared readings from both sources before the "breaking of the bread." The Second Vatican Council teaches that the Liturgy of the Word and the Liturgy of the Eucharist "are so closely connected with each other that they form but one single act of worship" (*Sacrosantum Concilium*, 56).

The Liturgy of the Word for Sunday Masses operates on a three-year cycle, named A, B, and C. Over the course of three years a good portion of the entire Bible will be read and heard on Sundays. The Gospel is the central focus of each set of readings. Its theme is woven together with the first reading. An important part of the Liturgy of the Word is the homily in which the priest or deacon explains the Word of God and exhorts those assembled to be open to accepting it and living it.

Jesus Christ is the one single Word of God. Through all of sacred scripture, God the Father speaks just one single Word, and that Word is Christ, who reveals the Father perfectly. The Church finds nourishment from the Word of God and takes care to meditate on this gift not as human words "but, as it truly is, the word of God, which is now at work in you who believe" (1 Thes 2:13).

*We center ourselves in Christ's presence and learn to hear him speak to us. Pope Benedict XVI said that "those who listen to the word of God and refer to it always, are constructing their existence on solid foundations" (*Message on the 21st World Youth Day*).*

Adoration and Sacrifice

The very words spoken by the priest during the Liturgy of the Eucharist (quoting Jesus from the Last Supper) indicate the sacrificial nature of Christ's offering. He says: "This is my Body, which will be given up for you." To "give up" indicates the offering of his body. Next, the priest says: "This is the chalice of my blood, . . . which will be poured out for you." The "pouring out" of Jesus's blood is his sacrifice for the forgiveness of our sins.

"The sacrifice of Christ and the sacrifice of the Eucharist are *one single sacrifice*" (*Catechism of the Catholic Church*, 1367). Jesus, who first offered himself on Calvary, now offers himself on the altar during the Liturgy of the Eucharist. On the Cross, Jesus's sacrifice was bloody; in the Mass, his sacrifice is unbloody because he now lives in his glorified state in heaven.

Following the words of institution in the Eucharistic Prayer, several prayerful intercessions are offered—for example, for all those gathered at the Eucharist; for the pope, bishops, and all the clergy; for Catholics in need; and for the faithful deceased. These intercessory prayers remind us that the whole Church has a part in this sacrificial meal in the hope of being brought together in unity with the entire family of God. When we say "Amen" at the end of the Eucharistic Prayer, we are professing our belief in all that was spoken and in our commitment to continue to share and practice this belief when Mass ends.

Jesus said, "For whoever wishes to save his life will lose it, but whoever loses his life for my sake and that of the gospel will save it" (Mk 8:35). Our time in Eucharistic Adoration is in itself a sacrifice of our time and our will. We ponder even bigger ways we must give up our own will and desires for Christ.

Adoration and Service

The Concluding Rites of Mass are short and simple. The priest or deacon may say, "Go forth, the Mass is ended." Or he may say, "Go and announce the Gospel of the Lord!" The message of the Concluding Rite is that because of the Eucharist you have just celebrated, the Lord is both with you and within you. His sanctifying grace empowers you to go forth and to be Eucharist for others. You have been commissioned not only to spread the Good News of Jesus with your words but also with your actions in service of others.

St. John Paul II explained that incorporation into Christ in Baptism is "constantly renewed and consolidated by sharing the Eucharistic Sacrifice" and that, when you celebrate Eucharist, you become a "'sacrament' for humanity . . . light of the world and salt of the earth . . . for the redemption of all" (*Ecclesia de Eucharistia*, 22). The Eucharist sends you out into the world ready to love and serve more completely. The Eucharist strengthens the bonds between all who receive it and makes it possible for you to demonstrate to yourself the love you are called to share with others.

We are renewed by our time with the Lord at Mass. Our tanks have been filled with God's grace, and we are inspired to bring love, care, mercy, peace, as well as concrete items of food, water, and clothing to those in need. Do we need to "top off our tanks" to activate such service? Time before the Blessed Sacrament provides a refresher.

How to Make a Holy Hour around the Four Elements of the Mass

Making a holy hour is both as simple and as difficult as committing one hour to spend before the Lord in the Blessed Sacrament. It is simple, recalling the words and actions of St. John Vianney who said, "I look at him and he looks at me." It is also difficult: "Could you not keep watch for one hour?" (Mk 14:37).

The *Ave Guide to Eucharistic Adoration* provides several ways to divide a personal holy hour into four fifteen-minute segments based on the four elements of Mass:

- Penance
- Word

- Sacrifice

- Service

Each of these four elements has reflections in *four different categories*:

- Prayers and Devotions

- Sacred Writings and Sacred Readings

- Saints and Faithful Disciples

- Doctrines and Teachings

Each of the reflections has a short introduction, a reading, and a suggestion for personal conversation with Jesus.

Sample Plans for a Holy Hour

You can organize your holy hour around each of the four elements of Mass, or focus on just one element of Mass (e.g., "Penance" or "Service"). You can also organize a holy hour around a particular category of reflection (e.g., "Prayers and Devotions" or "Saints and Faithful Disciples"). Or you can organize your holy hour around a combination of the four elements of Mass and the four categories of reflections.

Note four sample plans among many options for organizing a holy hour:

Focus on Penance

Penance	Word	Sacrifice	Service
Prayers and Devotions (page 2)	Prayers and Devotions	Prayers and Devotions	Prayers and Devotions
Sacred Writings and Sacred Readings (page 8)	Sacred Writings and Sacred Readings	Sacred Writings and Sacred Readings	Sacred Writings and Sacred Readings
Saints and Faithful Disciples (page 14)	Saints and Faithful Disciples	Saints and Faithful Disciples	Saints and Faithful Disciples
Doctrines and Teachings (page 24)	Doctrines and Teachings	Doctrines and Teachings	Doctrines and Teachings

Focus on Service

Penance	Word	Sacrifice	Service
Prayers and Devotions	Prayers and Devotions	Prayers and Devotions	Prayers and Devotions (page 114)
Sacred Writings and Sacred Readings	Sacred Writings and Sacred Readings	Sacred Writings and Sacred Readings	Sacred Writings and Sacred Readings (page 121)
Saints and Faithful Disciples	Saints and Faithful Disciples	Saints and Faithful Disciples	Saints and Faithful Disciples (page 128)
Doctrines and Teachings	Doctrines and Teachings	Doctrines and Teachings	Doctrines and Teachings (page 137)

Focus on Parts of Mass through Prayers and Devotions

Penance	Word	Sacrifice	Service
Prayers and Devotions (page 2)	Prayers and Devotions (page 36)	Prayers and Devotions (page 74)	Prayers and Devotions (page 114)
Sacred Writings and Sacred Readings	Sacred Writings and Sacred Readings	Sacred Writings and Sacred Readings	Sacred Writings and Sacred Readings
Saints and Faithful Disciples	Saints and Faithful Disciples	Saints and Faithful Disciples	Saints and Faithful Disciples
Doctrines and Teachings	Doctrines and Teachings	Doctrines and Teachings	Doctrines and Teachings

Focus on Elements of Mass through a Variety of Reflections

Penance	Word	Sacrifice	Service
Prayers and Devotions (page 2)	Prayers and Devotions	Prayers and Devotions	Prayers and Devotions
Sacred Writings and Sacred Readings	Sacred Writings and Sacred Readings (page 44)	Sacred Writings and Sacred Readings	Sacred Writings and Sacred Readings
Saints and Faithful Disciples	Saints and Faithful Disciples	Saints and Faithful Disciples (page 90)	Saints and Faithful Disciples
Doctrines and Teachings	Doctrines and Teachings	Doctrines and Teachings	Doctrines and Teachings (page 137)

Sample Holy Hour

Begin each holy hour with a prayer asking Jesus to accompany you in mind and heart.

Opening Prayer to Jesus

Come, Lord Jesus, be with me in this hour.
You said to your disciples, "My flesh is true food, and
    my blood is true drink" (Jn 6:55).
Some walked away from you on hearing your words.
Here I am, Lord.
I believe with all my heart that you are present in the
    Blessed Sacrament.
I believe that you have the words of eternal life.
Look at me, Lord.
Cast out of my heart all outside distractions.
I promise to look at you and listen to you speak to me.
I pray this in your name.
Amen.

Using the Reflections

Each "box" contains four reflections. Choose one reflection to focus on for fifteen minutes of your holy hour. Then follow these four steps.

1. Read the reflection introduction.

2. Read the reflection. Think about its meaning. What words or sentences stand out to you? What questions do you have about what you read?

3. Read the reflection a second time. Sit in silence with Jesus, thinking about what he might be saying to you in these words.

4. Read and pray with one or more of the suggestions from the Personal Conversation with Jesus.

Then move on to the next fifteen-minute "box" you have chosen and repeat the same process. Each time you make a holy hour, choose a different sample plan and a different set of reflections. End your holy hour with a closing prayer.

Closing Prayer to Jesus

Behold, Lamb of God.
Behold you, Jesus, who takes away my sins.
Happy am I when I am with you.
Happy am I to accept your mercy.
Happy am I to be loved by you.
Thank you, Jesus.
Amen.

Adoration and Penance

"The human heart is heavy and hardened. God must give man a new heart" (*Catechism of the Catholic Church*, 1432). God always gives us the strength to recalibrate our lives and begin again. We participate in this process when we have the resolve to accept God's grace of conversion. What better place to seek a change of heart than before Christ in the Blessed Sacrament? When we ask for God's forgiveness, we begin the process of a penitent—that is, one who admits his or her sins, who is truly sorry for having sinned, and who wishes to be restored to right relationship with God and the Church.

The Confiteor

The Confiteor (Latin for "I confess") is one of the prayers that can be said as part of the Penitential Act at Mass. When mentioning our faults, we strike our breasts three times. St. Augustine of Hippo said: "No sooner have you heard the word 'Confiteor,' than you strike your breast. What does this mean except that you wish to bring to light what is concealed in the breast, and by this act to cleanse your hidden sins?" (Sermo de verbis Domini, *13*).

> I confess to almighty God and to you, my brothers and sisters, that I have greatly sinned, in my thoughts and in my words, in what I have done, and in what I have failed to do; through my fault, through my fault, through my most grievous fault; therefore I ask blessed Mary ever-Virgin, all the Angels and Saints, and you, my brothers and sisters, to pray for me to the Lord our God.

Personal Conversation with Jesus

- Name occasions of sinful thoughts and words that have plagued you.

- When was a recent time you failed to do what was needed?

- Speak a prayer of sorrow to the Lord.

St. Faustina's Prayer for Sinners

This prayer is typically prayed at the opening of the Chaplet of Divine Mercy, a devotion linked to appearances of Christ to St. Faustina Kowalska, a Polish nun who lived in the early twentieth century and recorded in her diary (Diary, 72). The overall purpose of praying the chaplet is threefold: to obtain mercy, to trust in Christ's mercy, and to show mercy to others. (See appendix, page 150, for directions on praying the Chaplet of Divine Mercy.)

O Jesus, eternal Truth, our Life, I call upon You and I beg Your mercy for poor sinners. O sweetest Heart of my Lord, full of pity and unfathomable mercy, I plead with You for poor sinners. O Most Sacred Heart, Fount of Mercy from which gush forth rays of inconceivable graces upon the entire human race, I beg of You light for poor sinners. O Jesus, be mindful of Your own bitter Passion and do not permit the loss of souls redeemed at so dear a price of Your most precious Blood. O Jesus, when I consider the great price of Your Blood, I rejoice at its immensity, for one drop alone would have been enough for the salvation of all sinners. Although sin is an abyss of wickedness and ingratitude, the price paid for us can never be equaled. Therefore, let every soul trust in the Passion of the Lord, and place its hope in His mercy. God will not deny His mercy to anyone. Heaven and earth may change, but God's mercy will never be exhausted. Oh, what immense joy burns in my heart when I contemplate Your incomprehensible goodness, O Jesus! I desire to bring all sinners to Your feet that they may glorify Your mercy throughout endless ages.

Personal Conversation with Jesus

- Jesus is "full of pity and unfathomable mercy." How are these qualities comparable to each other?

- Contemplate what one drop of Jesus's blood has accomplished.

- Name a way you can show mercy to another in the next twenty-four hours.

My Nature Is Fire

St. Catherine of Siena (1347–1341) was an "advisor of the pope" personally in her life and has been ever since in her writings. Her ability to offer wise counsel and settle disputes that rocked the papacy led to her canonization in 1461. Pope St. Paul VI gave her the title of Doctor of the Church in 1970. This prayer, tucked within her many writings, calls us to recognize the gift of our God-given nature that is absent of sin.

In your nature, eternal Godhead,
I shall come to know my nature.
And what is my nature, boundless love?
It is fire,
because you are nothing but a fire of
    love.
And you have given humankind
a share in this nature,
for by the fire of love you created us.
And so with all other people
and every created thing;
you made them out of love.
O ungrateful people!
What nature has your God given you?
His very own nature!
Are you not ashamed to cut yourself off
    from such a noble thing

through the guilt of deadly sin?
O eternal Trinity, my sweet love!
You, light, give us light.
You, wisdom, give us wisdom.
You, supreme strength, strengthen us.
Today, eternal God,
let our cloud be dissipated
so that we may perfectly know and fol-
    low your Truth in truth,
with a free and simple heart.
God, come to our assistance!
Lord, make haste to help us!
Amen.

Personal Conversation with Jesus

- Imagine the holy nature God intends for you. What is it like?

- Share with Jesus something you are grateful for.

- Tell Jesus how you will be on fire for him.

Act of Contrition

Contrition is heartfelt sorrow for sins committed, along with the intention of sinning no more. Perfect contrition arises from your love for God and your desire to be in relationship with him. It is also called "contrition of charity," and it obtains forgiveness from mortal sins as long as it is accompanied by recourse to the Sacrament of Penance as soon as possible. Imperfect contrition, or "attrition," is sorrow for sin because you fear punishment or perceive the ugliness of your sin. It is also valid in the celebration of the Sacrament of Penance.

O my God, I am heartily sorry for having offended Thee, and I detest all my sins because of Thy just punishment, but most of all because they offend Thee, my God, who art all good and deserving of all my love. I firmly resolve with the help of Thy grace to sin no more and to avoid the near occasion of sin. Amen.

Personal Conversation with Jesus

- Is your heartfelt sorrow for your sins perfect or imperfect?

- In what particular ways do your sins offend God, others, and yourself?

- Tell Jesus of your resolution not to sin again. Ask for his grace to help with this promise.

Joel 2:12–13

The Book of Joel was one of the last prophetic books of the Old Testament, completed in roughly 400 BC. Joel's message was a call to repentance and fasting, after which he promised God would bless the people. The prophet refers to a "day of the Lord" when God would battle all the evil forces of the world.

> Yet even now—oracle of the LORD—
> > return to me with your whole heart,
> > with fasting, weeping, and mourning.
> Rend your hearts, not your garments,
> > and return to the LORD, your God,
> For he is gracious and merciful,
> > slow to anger, abounding in steadfast love,
> > and relenting in punishment.

Personal Conversation with Jesus

- "Return to me," says the Lord. How have you been absent from God?

- Which sins do you weep over? Bring those to Jesus.

- God's love for you has been steadfast. Name a way this has been true for you despite your remaining absent from him.

Psalm 32:1-6a

This is one of seven Penitential Psalms. The psalmist writes from his own experience of being stubborn to the Lord's call to repent and of being subject to sin's power. The consequence of sinful behavior without repentance is understood as frustration and the waning of one's vitality.

Blessed is the one whose fault is removed,
    whose sin is forgiven.
Blessed is the one to whom the LORD imputes
    no guilt,
    in whose spirit is no deceit.

Because I kept silent, my bones wasted away;
    I groaned all day long.
For day and night your hand was heavy upon me;
    my strength withered as in dry summer heat.
      Selah
Then I declared my sin to you;
    my guilt I did not hide.
I said, "I confess my transgression to the LORD,"
    and you took away the guilt of my sin.
      Selah
Therefore every loyal person should pray to you
    in time of distress.

Personal Conversation with Jesus

- What is a sin you have been silent about for quite a bit of time? Tell Jesus about the sin.

- How has your physical well-being been impacted by sin?

- Share your joy about being forgiven.

Romans 6:1-11

In Baptism, we have died to sin. We also share in the death of sin and escape the oppression of sin that weighs us down in this life. Our salvation will be complete in the future when we share in Christ's Resurrection. St. Paul, in the Letter to the Romans, makes the point that if we have been baptized and likewise care about our future, we will have little motivation to continue with our sinful behavior.

What then shall we say? Shall we persist in sin that grace may abound? Of course not! How can we who died to sin yet live in it? Or are you unaware that we who were baptized into Christ Jesus were baptized into his death? We were indeed buried with him through baptism into death, so that, just as Christ was raised from the dead by the glory of the Father, we too might live in newness of life.

For if we have grown into union with him through a death like his, we shall also be united with him in the resurrection. We know that our old self was crucified with him, so that our sinful body might be done away with, that we might no longer be in slavery to sin. For a dead person has been absolved from sin. If, then, we have died with Christ, we believe that we shall also live with him. We know that Christ raised from the dead, dies no more; death no longer has power of him. As to his death, he died to sin once and for all; as to his life, he lives for God. Consequently, you too must think of yourselves as [being] dead to sin and living for God in Christ Jesus.

Personal Conversation with Jesus

- Who brought you to the Church for Baptism? How do you see Jesus in this person(s)?

- What motivates you to refrain from sinning?

- Make a promise to Jesus about incorporating your life more fully with his.

Matthew 9:10-13

Jesus taught that mercy is superior to sacrifice. In the Sermon on the Mount, he said that those who show mercy will be treated with mercy. Mercy urges empathy. We are to think, feel, and act from another's perspective rather than our own. The words in this passage were directed to the Pharisees who complained that Jesus was eating with tax collectors and sinners rather than with those whom they considered the righteous.

> While [Jesus] was at table in [Matthew's] house, many tax collectors and sinners came and sat with Jesus and his disciples. The Pharisees saw this and said to the disciples, "Why does your teacher eat with tax collectors and sinners?" [Jesus] heard this and said, "Those who are well do not need a physician, but the sick do. Go and learn the meaning of the words, 'I desire mercy, not sacrifice.' I did not come to call the righteous but sinners."

Personal Conversation with Jesus

- Ask Jesus what he means about his preference for mercy over sacrifice and how you should apply the lesson in your own life.

- Who is a "sinner" you must forgive?

- Where can you go to learn how to be merciful?

Immaculée Ilibagiza: "I Forgive You"

Immaculée Ilibagiza was born in 1972 in Rwanda, a relatively small French-speaking nation (and former colony of Belgium) in central sub-Saharan Africa. In April 1994, when Immaculée was in her early twenties, civil unrest quickly escalated to what has come to be known as the Rwandan genocide.

Members of the Hutu tribe began targeting and massacring members of the Tutsi tribe. Immaculée and her family, as Tutsis, were in mortal danger. Sadly, most of Immaculée's immediate family—including both of her parents and two of her brothers (a third brother was studying in Senegal)—were killed in one of the violent raids. Immaculée was able to escape and went into hiding with other Tutsi women in the cramped bathroom of a family friend. She remained in this space for ninety-one days. During that time, her weight dropped from 115 pounds to just 65 pounds.

The home's owner provided the women with as much food as he could without appearing suspicious. During this ordeal, with the constant threat that they might be discovered by the marauding Hutu troops, who frequently searched the neighboring homes, Immaculée prayed fervently and silently, including the Rosary, for hours every day. During the women's captivity, Immaculée also began learning English with nothing but a Bible and a French-English dictionary.

In July 1994, French soldiers arrived in Rwanda, bringing an end to the massacre and securing a level of peace and stability by supporting a new government. The ultimate total of the genocide was overwhelming: around one million innocent Tutsis, along with Hutus who aided their Tutsi countrymen, were killed in the Rwandan genocide. It remains one of the deadliest conflicts of the modern era. Immaculée Ilibagiza was afraid that this dreadful experience would leave her forever bitter and wounded. Instead, she emerged from captivity with a willingness to forgive. She came face-to-face with the killer of her mother and was able to utter the words "I forgive you."

Immaculée has also encouraged reconciliation and forgiveness for those who were responsible for carrying out the Rwandan genocide. She shared these words in her book Led by Faith: Rising from the Ashes of the Rwandan Genocide *(Hay House, 2009):*

> I said the Lord's Prayer hundreds of times, hoping to forgive the killers who were murdering all around me. It was no use. Every time I got to the part asking God to "forgive those who trespass against us," my mouth went dry. I couldn't say the words because I didn't truly embrace the feeling behind them. My inability to forgive caused me even greater pain than the anguish I felt in being separated from my family, and it was worse than the physical torment of being constantly hunted.

Personal Conversation with Jesus

- Imagine how Jesus felt forgiving those who put him to death.

- How does the inability to forgive cause you anguish?

- Which do you find more difficult to forgive: an individual or a group? Tell Jesus about each situation.

Bl. Henry Suso: God's Love for the Sinner

Bl. Henry Suso was a mystic, preacher, and author of the fourteenth century. Born to a noble family of Berg in Germany, he entered the Dominican convent when he was thirteen years old. Even in religious life, Henry was careless and not attentive to his spiritual formation. He had a further conversion when he was eighteen, making himself "the Servant of Eternal Wisdom." He devoted his life from that point forward to a fiery love to meditate on the perfection of God and God's plan for humans. His mystical thoughts were recorded in sermons and letters.

Henry's spiritual growth was noted by a practice that he gave up as he grew older. Early in his life, Henry subjected himself to painful mortifications as penance for his sins. For example, he wore undergarments studded with 150 brass nails. He also slept on a door with thirty protruding nails that he laid on the ground. As he matured, he concluded that the mortifications were actually distractions from his loving God more deeply. He came to recognize the mercy of God, rather than viewing him as a God of judgment and punishment.

> No mother could snatch her child from a burning building more swiftly than God is constrained to succor a penitent soul, even though it should have committed every sin in the world a thousand times over.

Personal Conversation with Jesus

- Do you ever think of yourself as unforgivable?

- Who has forgiven you multiple times?

- Examine your conscience as preparation for celebrating the Sacrament of Penance as soon as possible.

St. John Vianney: "Put Yourself on Good Terms with God"

The Curé of Ars or "Priest of Ars" is the name given to St. John Vianney, who was assigned to this remote parish well outside of Paris shortly after his ordination in 1815. When he arrived, he found that the people there had given up their practice of the faith in the time since the French Revolution. Fr. Vianney began his ministry by helping those most in need: those who were sick or housebound. He helped destitute girls by gathering them together into an orphanage called Providence. His catechism lessons and lectures to the girls became so popular that parishioners came to hear them and, eventually, they had to be moved to the church.

Fr. Vianney encouraged his parishioners to return to the Sacrament of Penance. He took time with each penitent when they did come, offering words of compassion and healing before giving them absolution from their sins. Fr. Vianney commonly spent fifteen to eighteen hours a day in the confessional. His biographers estimate that he heard tens of thousands of Confessions over his lifetime. Before long, so many people from all over France came to him for Confession that the French railroad had to open a special ticket office in Lyons (the nearest city) just to accommodate passengers to Ars. It became known among the pilgrims that St. John Vianney could "read hearts" and also had the gift of healing. He connected a person's good Confession to "taking the nails out of Jesus." The simple man who was sent to an obscure village is now the patron saint of parish priests.

It is a beautiful thought, my children, that we have a Sacrament which heals the wounds of our soul! My children, we cannot comprehend the goodness of God towards us in instituting this great Sacrament of Penance. If we had had a favor to ask of Our Lord, we should never have thought of asking him that. But he foresaw our frailty and our inconstancy in well-doing, and his love induced him to do what we should not have dared to ask. My children, if someone has a serious illness, he must have the doctor; after the doctor come the remedies. In the same way, when we have fallen into any grievous sin, we must have recourse to the doctor, that is the priest; and to the remedy, that is confession.

Personal Conversation with Jesus

- Jesus says, "Tell me your sins."
- What keeps you from the Sacrament of Penance?
- Share with Jesus your own prayer of sorrow.

St. John Paul II: "The Gospel of Life"

St. John Paul II's eleventh encyclical, Evangelium Vitae *(The Gospel of Life), was absolutely clear in naming the most important human right: the right to life. The pope clearly addressed specific attacks against human life, such as euthanasia, capital punishment . . . and abortion. St. John Paul II wrote that "abortion and euthanasia are thus crimes which no human law can claim to legitimize" (73).*

Yet, the pope recognized prevailing factors in modern society that lead to many women making the choice of abortion. (Two of the most prominent are the breakdown of family life and a belief in freedom as an absolute value.) In any case, abortion is also devastating to the mother, who is often forced into such a choice. In Evangelium Vitae *(99), St. John Paul addressed women who have had abortion in this way:*

> I would now like to say a special word to women who have had an abortion. The Church is aware of the many factors which may have influenced your decision, and she does not doubt that in many cases it was a painful and even shattering decision. The wound in your heart may not yet have healed. Certainly what happened was and remains terribly wrong. But do not give in to discouragement and do not lose hope. Try rather to understand what happened

and face it honestly. If you have not already done so, give yourselves over with humility and trust to repentance. The Father of mercies is ready to give you his forgiveness and his peace in the Sacrament of Reconciliation. To the same Father and to his mercy you can with sure hope entrust your child. With the friendly and expert help and advice of other people, and as a result of your own painful experience, you can be among the most eloquent defenders of everyone's right to life. Through your commitment to life, whether by accepting the birth of other children or by welcoming and caring for those most in need of someone to be close to them, you will become promoters of a new way of looking at human life.

Personal Conversation with Jesus

- Pray for the children lost in abortion.
- Speak with Jesus for consolation and forgiveness for anyone you know who has had an abortion and all women in general who have had an abortion.

- Who is someone in material, emotional, or spiritual need in your family or community? Bring this person to Jesus in prayer.

Catechism of the Catholic Church: Forgive as Our Heavenly Father Forgives

There are several conditions that accompany the reconciliation we seek with God and among our brothers and sisters. We can't be reconciled with God unless he forgives us. We can't be forgiven by God unless we forgive others. We can't be reconciled with others unless we forgive them. Others can't reconcile with us unless they also forgive us.

The Catechism of the Catholic Church *(2845), quoting St. Cyprian, reminds us that we are always debtors and that we owe everyone we encounter—friends and enemies alike—our love.*

> There is no limit or measure to this essentially divine forgiveness, whether one speaks of "sins" as in Luke (11:4), "debts" as in Matthew (6:12). We are always debtors: "Owe no one anything, except to love one another." The communion of the Holy Trinity is the source and criterion of truth in every relationship. It is lived out in prayer, above all in the Eucharist.
>
> God does not accept the sacrifice of a sower of disunion, but commands that he depart from the altar so that he may first be reconciled with his brother. For

God can be appeased only by prayers that make peace. To God, the better offering is peace, brotherly concord, and a people made one in the unity of the Father, Son, and Holy Spirit.

Personal Conversation with Jesus

- Imagine the relationship among the Divine Persons of the Holy Trinity. What is it like?

- Where is disunity in your life?

- Talk with Jesus about someone whom you might consider an "enemy" and someone else who might consider you an "enemy." What is the path to reconciliation with these two people?

Evangelii Gaudium: Lift Up Your Head and Start Anew!

The 2013 apostolic exhortation by Pope Francis, Evangelii Gaudium *(The Joy of the Gospel), is representative of so many of the themes of Pope Francis's papacy, especially a call to reform our lives and understand ourselves as disciples who are "permanently in a state of mission" to share the Good News of Jesus Christ. In this passage from the opening of* Evangelii Gaudium *(3), Pope Francis invites us to return to Jesus, to come into a personal encounter with him, and to not be held back by any sinful decisions in our past.*

I invite all Christians, everywhere, at this very moment, to a renewed personal encounter with Jesus Christ, or at least an openness to letting him encounter them; I ask all of you to do this unfailingly each day. No one should think that this invitation is not meant for him or her, since "no one is excluded from the joy brought by the Lord." The Lord does not disappoint those who take this risk; whenever we take a step towards Jesus, we come to realize that he is already there, waiting for us with open arms. Now is the time to say to Jesus: "Lord, I have let myself be deceived; in a thousand ways I have shunned your love, yet here I am once more, to renew my covenant with you. I need you. Save me once again, Lord, take me once more into your redeeming embrace." How good it feels to come back to him whenever we are lost! Let me say this once more: God never tires of forgiving us; we are the ones who tire of seeking his mercy. Christ, who told us to forgive one another "seventy times seven" (Mt 18:22) has given us his example: he has forgiven us seventy times seven. Time and time again he bears us on his shoulders. No one can strip us of the dignity bestowed upon us by this boundless and unfailing love. With a tenderness which never disappoints, but is always capable of restoring our joy, he makes it possible for us to lift up our heads and to start anew. Let us not flee from the resurrection of Jesus, let us never give up, come what will.

May nothing inspire more than his life,
which impels us onwards.

Personal Conversation with Jesus

- Tell Jesus about yourself in depth.

- Repeat the sentence beginning with "Lord, I have let myself be deceived" from Pope Francis's address, and say it directly to Jesus.

- Tell Jesus about the most joyful time of your life. How can that joy be restored and made new again?

Letter 180 of Pope St. Leo the Great: The Remedy of Sin Is the Sacrament of Penance

St. Leo the Great was pope during the fifth century when Attila the Hun was marching toward Rome and pillaging each town across the countryside that his army traveled. Pope Leo is famously known for negotiating an agreement face-to-face with Attila that spared the city of Rome. Yet, Pope Leo did much more. He preached instructive homilies, of which nearly one hundred are still preserved in writing. He also wrote hundreds of personal letters that amplified many truths of the faith. In Letter 180, he writes of the necessity of the Sacrament of Penance for anyone who sins after Baptism and how Christ is the minister who accompanies the penitent and priest in offering absolution from sins.

The manifold mercy of God so assists men when they fall, that not only by the grace of Baptism but also by the remedy of penitence is the hope of eternal life revived, in order that they who have violated the gifts of the second birth, condemning themselves by their own judgment, may attain to remission of their crimes, the provisions of the Divine Goodness having so ordained that God's indulgence cannot be obtained without the supplications of priests. For the Mediator between God and men, the Man Christ Jesus, has transmitted this power to those that are set over the Church that they should both grant a course of penitence to those who confess, and, when they are cleansed by wholesome correction admit them through the door of reconciliation to communion in the sacraments. In which work assuredly the Saviour Himself unceasingly takes part and is never absent from those things, the carrying out of which He has committed to His ministers, saying: "Lo, I am with you all the days even to the completion of the age" (Mt 28:20): so that whatever is accomplished through our service in due order and with satisfactory results we doubt not to have been vouchsafed through the Holy Spirit.

Personal Conversation with Jesus

- Why do you need the Sacrament of Penance?
- When will you go to Confession?
- Ask Jesus to be with you when you go to Confession.

General Instruction of the Roman Missal: The Penitential Act

In the Penitential Act at Mass we confess our sins. One of the forms begins with "I confess to almighty God, and to you, my brothers and sisters, that I have greatly sinned." After we say these words, the priest offers us absolution from our venial sins. A venial sin is a sin that weakens our relationship with God but does not destroy the grace in our soul. The absolution offered in the Penitential Act does not remove mortal sins from our souls, though it does protect us against future mortal sins. A mortal sin is a serious, deadly violation of God's law of love that destroys sanctifying grace in our souls. Mortal sins involve grave matter, full knowledge of the evil done, and consent of will. God grants forgiveness of mortal sins only through the Sacrament of Penance. The following text is from the Introductory Rites subsection (paragraphs 51–52).

After [the greeting], the Priest calls upon the whole community to take part in the Penitential Act, which, after a brief pause for silence, it does by means of a formula of general confession. The rite concludes with the Priest's absolution, which, however, lacks the efficacy of the Sacrament of Penance.

From time to time on Sundays, especially in Easter Time, instead of the customary Penitential Act, the blessing and sprinkling of water may take place as a reminder of Baptism.

After the Penitential Act, the *Kyrie, eleison* (Lord, have mercy), is always begun, unless it has already been part of the Penitential Act. Since it is a chant by which the faithful acclaim the Lord and implore his mercy, it is usually executed by everyone, that is to say, with the people and the choir or cantor taking part in it.

Personal Conversation with Jesus

- Think about a time when someone apologized to you. How did you offer forgiveness?

- Offer the Lord sorrow for your personal sins and the sins of the world.

- Thank Jesus for the gift of his mercy.

Adoration and Word

The Mass is a dialogue between the priest and the people. At various parts of the Mass, we give our consent to the words the priest speaks on our behalf by saying "Amen" or "I agree." We are not passive listeners to the readings from sacred scripture during the Liturgy of the Word either. We listen attentively and then respond, "Thanks be to God," and, to the Gospel, "Praise to you, Lord Jesus Christ." Likewise, when we are at Eucharistic Adoration, we dialogue with Jesus. We listen attentively to him in our personal thoughts. We also share in the words that he has spoken to us in the Bible and that are proclaimed at Mass. "Through all the words of Sacred Scripture, God speaks only one single Word, his one Utterance in whom he expresses completely" (*Catechism of the Catholic Church*, 101). That Word is Jesus Christ.

The Gloria

*The beautiful Gloria ("Glory to God") prayed during the Introductory Rites of Mass, before the collect, recalls the Incarnation, when God the Father, despite our sinfulness, sent his Son to be our Savior. The Gloria is really a doxology—that is, an expression of praise to God. The Gloria is known as the "greater doxology" in distinction from the shorter Glory Be prayer. The Gloria has roots in the Gospel of Luke, where three times a hymn is sung in giving glory to the Son of God: at the announcement of the birth of Jesus (Lk 1:29), in the Magnificat (Lk 1:46–55; pages 40–41), and in Simeon's canticle at the presentation of Jesus in the Temple (Lk 2:29–32). Pope Benedict XVI said of the Gloria, "The Church, in the Gloria, has extended this song of praise, which the angels sang in response to the event of the holy night, into a hymn of joy at God's glory" (*2010 Solemnity of the Nativity of the Lord Homily).

Glory to God in the highest. And on earth peace to men of good will. We praise You. We bless You. We adore you. We glorify You. We give You thanks for Your great glory. O Lord God, heavenly King, God the Father almighty. O Lord Jesus Christ, the Only-begotten Son. O Lord God, Lamb of God, Son of the Father: you Who take away the sins of the world, have mercy on us. You Who take away the sins of the world, receive our prayer. You Who sit at the right hand of the Father, have mercy on us. For you alone are holy. You alone are the Lord. You alone, O Jesus Christ, are most high. Together with the Holy Spirit in the glory of God the Father. Amen.

Personal Conversation with Jesus

- Praise, adore, and thank God the Father, the King of the Universe, for sending his Son to be our Savior.

- Contemplate the relationship between Father, Son, and Holy Spirit.

- Repeat a mantra: "Receive my prayer, O Lord."

Praying the Our Father Using Lectio Divina

Prayer is the key ingredient to grow in friendship with Jesus. The Bible is the source for prayer as well as for a method of praying called lectio div- ina, *or "divine reading." You can also think of lectio divina as "prayerful reading." St. Benedict of Clairvaux in the sixth century left instructions in his Rule of St. Benedict for doing divine reading. His instructions can be divided into three steps:*

- *The first step, lectio (reading), involves selecting a spiritual reading, in this case, scripture. Once you select a passage, you are to read the passage until a verse or phrase strikes you. At this point, you are to stop and begin your meditation.*

- *The second step, meditatio (meditation), asks you to pause and to let the meaning of the words sink into your mind and heart. Mentally repeat the words over and over again. Let them become part of you. Appreciate what they are saying. After spending some time pondering the meaning of the words, you turn to the prayer.*

- *The third step, oratio, is from the Latin word for "prayer." In this step, you speak to God about the phrase, or simply sit in God's presence and let him speak to you. When you find that you have exhausted your prayer, or when you become distracted, return to the passage again and begin to read until you come to another phrase that seems to be speaking directly to you. Then continue the process as before.*

- *Try praying using lectio divina with the prayer that Jesus taught us.*

> Our Father, who art in heaven,
> hallowed be thy name;
> thy kingdom come,
> thy will be done
> on earth as it is in heaven.
> Give us this day our daily bread,
> and forgive our trespasses,
> as we forgive those who trespass against
>   us;
> And lead us not into temptation,
> but deliver us from evil.
> Amen.

Personal Conversation with Jesus

- Imagine yourself with the disciples who heard Jesus teach them how to pray this way.

- Which part of the prayer made you pause and ponder more deeply?

- How do you imagine God as "Father"?

The Magnificat

The Magnificat (Latin for "magnifies") is an ancient Marian hymn and, in fact, perhaps the most ancient Marian hymn. It is recorded in Luke 1:46–55. Like other biblical canticles or songs in Luke's gospel (for example, Zechariah's Benedictus in 1:68–79; pages 119–120), the Magnificat has the form of a hymn of praise found in the Old Testament. The words in the Magnificat are ascribed to Mary.

My soul proclaims the greatness of the Lord;
> my spirit rejoices in God my savior.

For he has looked upon his handmaid's lowliness;
> behold, from now on will all ages call me blessed.

The Mighty One has done great things for me,
> and holy is his name.

His mercy is from age to age
> to those who fear him.

He has shown might with his arm,
> dispersed the arrogant of mind and heart.

He has thrown down the rulers from their thrones
> but lifted up the lowly.

The hungry he has filled with good things;
> the rich he has sent away empty.

He has helped Israel his servant,
> remembering his mercy,

according to his promise to our fathers,
to Abraham and to his descendants forever.

Personal Conversation with Jesus

- Ask Jesus about his love for his mother.

- How has God always been faithful to you?

- What daily actions show that you rejoice in the Lord?

The Fraction Rite

The Fraction Rite is the part of the Mass when the priest breaks the sacred host. This action symbolizes that Christ's Body was broken for us so that when we receive Holy Communion we will be one with him and one another. During the Fraction Rite, the priest also drops a small piece of the sacred host into the chalice to signify the unity of the Body and Blood of Jesus in the work of salvation. The familiar prayer during the Fraction Rite is the Angus Dei ("Lamb of God"), which is based on John the Baptist's words when he saw Jesus come toward him ("Behold, the Lamb of God, who takes away the sin of the world" [Jn 1:29]). The priest then holds up the host and we have the opportunity to adore. Our response echoes the words of the Roman centurion with an ill servant who did not feel his home was worthy enough to welcome Jesus inside.

> Lamb of God, you take away the sins of the world, have mercy on us.
> Lamb of God, you take away the sins of the world, have mercy on us.
> Lamb of God, you take away the sins of the world, grant us peace.
> Behold the Lamb of God, behold him who takes away the sins of the world.
> Blessed are those called to the supper of the Lamb.

Lord, I am not worthy that you should enter under my roof, but only say the word and my soul shall be healed.

Personal Conversation with Jesus

- Tell Jesus about how you find strength in being broken.

- Behold Jesus in the Blessed Sacrament. Thank him for his gift of Real Presence.

- Ask Jesus to say the word so that your soul can be healed.

Isaiah 40:28-31

Chapters 40 to 54 of the Book of Isaiah are sometimes designated "Second Isaiah," as this section differs in its message from the first thirty-nine chapters. In this section, the prophet preaches a message to the Jewish exiles in Babylon, reminding them to be faithful to the Creator God and to use their captivity as a chance for repentance.

> Do you not know?
>> Have you not heard?
>
> The LORD is GOD from old,
>> creator of the ends of the earth.
>
> He does not faint or grow weary,
>> and his knowledge is beyond scrutiny.
>
> He gives power to the faint,
>> abundant strength to the weak.
>
> Though young men faint and grow weary,
>> and youths stagger and fall,
>
> They that hope in the LORD will renew their strength,
>> they will soar on eagles' wings;
>
> They will run and not grow weary,
>> walk and not grow faint.

Personal Conversation with Jesus

- How can you comprehend God never having a beginning?

- Ask the Lord to renew you in the strength to serve him.

- How do you want to soar with the Lord? Tell him.

Psalm 119:89-96

Psalm 119 is the longest in the entire Psalter. It praises God for giving his laws for people to live by. It also reflects the awe that God's Word has created the world and that his Word is faithful in sustaining the world and is unfailing.

Your word, LORD, stands forever;
　　it is firm as the heavens.
Through all generations your truth endures;
　　fixed to stand firm like the earth.
By your judgments they stand firm to this day,
　　for all things are your servants.
Had your law not been my delight,
　　I would have perished in my affliction.
I will never forget your precepts;
　　through them you give me life.
I am yours; save me,
　　for I cherish your precepts.
The wicked hope to destroy me,
　　but I seek to understand your testimonies.
I have seen the limits of all perfection,
　　but your commandment is without bounds.

Personal Conversation with Jesus

- Do you mainly struggle with God's laws or celebrate God's laws?

- What is a truth in your life that has endured?

- "Jesus, you are my strength." Repeat this mantra.

1 Peter 1:22-25

Christians are reborn through Christ. Those who accept the Gospel are guaranteed a new and lasting existence. A duty accompanies this rebirth: to love one another.

Since you have purified yourselves by obedience to the truth for sincere mutual love, love one another intensely from a [pure] heart. You have been born anew, not from perishable but from imperishable seed, through the living and abiding word of God, for:
"All flesh is like grass,
and all its glory like the flower of the field;
the grass withers,
and the flower wilts;
but the word of the Lord remains forever."
This is the word that has been proclaimed to you.

Personal Conversation with Jesus

- Imagine yourself spending eternity with Jesus.

- How can you live each day understanding that you are imperishable?

- What does your life look like born anew in the Lord?

John 1:1-5

This passage from the prologue of John's gospel is a poem that teaches that Jesus is the Word who is always present with God and who is always God. He has been God before creation since he has always existed. This passage speaks of the difference between the way God thinks and the way humans think. Your thoughts, even when you are remembering someone you know and love, are incomplete and sketchy. When God thinks, his thoughts are so complete that things come into existence. This passage is remindful of Genesis 1:3: "Let there be light"—and by the virtue of God thinking that, there is light.

> In the beginning was the Word,
> > and the Word was with God,
> > and the Word was God.
> He was in the beginning with God.
> All things came to be through him,
> > and without him nothing came to be.
> What came to be through him was life,
> > and this life was the light of the human race;
> the light shines in the darkness,
> > and the darkness has not overcome it.

Personal Conversation with Jesus

- Ask the Father to show you the Son.

- Think back on the last twenty-four hours. Share three times you recognized God's providence acting in your life.

- Let Jesus tell you how he provides light to your darkness.

St. Jerome:
Do Not Be Ignorant of Scripture

In the late fourth century, St. Jerome translated the Bible from its original languages into Latin, which became the Church's official Latin text for the next fifteen hundred years. Jerome was born in northeast Italy. He went to Rome as a young man to study Latin and Greek literature and had an early devotion to some non-Christian scholars. This education in the classics inspired him to a lifelong study. After being baptized at age eighteen, he entered a strict monastic community near his home at Aquileia. There, he mastered Hebrew. Returning to Rome, he was commissioned by Pope Damasus to translate the Bible. This task took him to Bethlehem, where he labored for twenty-three years, living mostly as an ascetic in a cave to complete his work.

*St. Jerome's work was a labor of love. He famously pointed out the importance of the Bible in growing in a deeper relationship with Jesus when he said that "ignorance of the Scriptures is ignorance of Christ." The Church echoes this, saying that it "forcefully and specifically exhorts all the Christian faithful . . . to learn the surpassing knowledge of Jesus Christ, by frequent reading of the divine Scriptures" (*Catechism of the Catholic Church, *133, quoting* Dei Verbum, *25).*

St. Jerome wrote dozens of letters advising popes and bishops on many topics, especially scripture. The following is an excerpt of a letter he wrote to Paulinus, the bishop of Nola.

In the apocalypse a book is shewn sealed with seven seals, which if you deliver to one that is learned saying, "Read this, he will answer you, I cannot, for it is sealed." How many there are today who fancy themselves learned, yet the scriptures are a sealed book to them, and one which they cannot open save through Him who has the key of David, "he that opens and no man shuts; and shuts and no man opens." In the Acts of the Apostles the holy eunuch (or rather "man" for so the scripture calls him) when reading Isaiah he is asked by Philip "Do you understand thou what you read?" makes answer: "How can I except some man should guide me?"

Although he had the book in his hand and took into his mind the words of the Lord, nay even had them on his tongue and uttered them with his lips, he still knew not Him, whom—not knowing—he worshipped in the book. Then Philip came and showed him Jesus, who was concealed beneath the letter. Wondrous excellence of the teacher! In the same hour the eunuch believed and was baptized; he became one of the faithful and a saint. He was no longer a pupil but a master; and he found more in the church's font there in the wilderness than he had ever done in the gilded temple of the synagogue.

Personal Conversation with Jesus

- What do you find hard to understand in the Bible?

- Pray to Jesus, asking him to unseal the words of scripture for you.

- Who is a mentor who can open the Word of God with you?

St. Gregory of Nyssa:
Let Scripture Guide You

St. Gregory of Nyssa was born in Caesarea, the capital of Cappadocia (central Turkey), in about 334. He, his brother St. Basil the Great, and their friend, St. Gregory of Nazianzus, are known collectively as the Cappadocian Fathers, who are credited with defining Christian orthodoxy in the Eastern Roman Empire. Gregory of Nyssa was a staunch defender of the faith against Arianism, which claimed that Christ was neither divine nor human, but something in between and only a created being. Gregory relied heavily on sacred scripture to repudiate Arianism. He wrote numerous commentaries and sermons on the Bible, and he is quoted here on his appreciation for sacred scripture.

> Just as in the sea those who are carried away from the direction of the harbor bring themselves back on course by a clear sign on seeing a tall beacon light or some mountain peak coming into view, so Scripture may guide those adrift on the sea of life back into the harbor of the divine will.

Personal Conversation with Jesus

- In what way are you adrift in life?

- What is a scripture passage over the course of your life that always centers you and reminds you of the love of God?

- Contemplate Jesus as a beacon of light directing you home. Describe this vision.

Madeleine L'Engle:
"The Bethlehem Explosion"

God's revelation of himself and his purpose is gradual. He has revealed himself in stages. Our salvation history is told in the pages of the Bible. First, God spoke to Adam and Eve and made a promise with them in Genesis 3:15 that he would send a Redeemer to defeat Satan and sin and restore humanity to perfection. After a series of covenants detailed in the Old Testament, God made himself most perfectly known through his Son, Jesus Christ.

Madeleine L'Engle (1918–2007) was a Christian writer who once said that it was her duty as a writer "to further the coming of the kingdom and to turn our feet toward home." In her poem "The Bethlehem Explosion" she writes about a common experiment in a chemistry class. Because she sees the world with the eyes of faith, this experiment becomes a sign and metaphor for the coming of Jesus in the world. She opens with a reference to the infancy narrative in the Gospel of Luke.

> In those days a decree went out from Caesar Augustus that the world should be enrolled. And Joseph too went up from the town of Nazareth to Judea, to the city of David that is called Bethlehem, because he was of the house and family of David, to be enrolled with Mary, his betrothed, who was with child (Lk 1:1, 4–5).

The chemistry lab at school
was in an old greenhouse
surrounded by ancient live oaks
garnished with Spanish moss.

The experiment I remember best
was pouring a quart of clear fluid
into a glass jar, and dropping into it,
grain by grain, salt-sized crystals,
until they layered
like white sand on the floor of the jar.

One more grain—and suddenly—
water and crystal burst
into a living, moving pattern,
a silent, quietly violent explosion.
The teacher told us that only when
we supersaturated the solution,
would come the precipitation.

The little town
was like the glass jar in our lab.
One by one they came, grain by grain,
all those of the house of David,
like grains of sand to be counted.

The inn was full. When Joseph knocked,

his wife was already in labor; there was
 no room
even for compassion. Until the barn was
 offered.
That was the precipitating factor. A
 child was born,
and the pattern changed forever, the
 cosmos
shaken with that silent explosion.

Personal Conversation with Jesus

- What aspects of the birth of Jesus are represented by the glass jar, the grains of crystal, and the silent and violent explosion in the glass jar?

- Tell Jesus how his birth revealed the dynamic love of God present from the beginning of creation.

- How has God gradually made himself known to you throughout your life?

St. Thérèse of Lisieux: The Little Flower

St. Thérèse of Lisieux, born in 1873 in France, entered the Carmelite convent when she was fifteen. She died of tuberculosis when she was twenty-four. When she was sick and at the insistence of two mother superiors, she wrote her life story and titled it The Story of a Soul. *It was completed shortly before she died. It has become one of the most widely read classics of spiritual life. The reason for the book's popularity and for the popularity of Thérèse herself is that she describes what most Christians would like to be: a person dedicated to the love of Jesus Christ. Thérèse also shows that to be a saint one doesn't have to be famous or to do something dramatic. She called her journey to God "the little way," a way in which the most ordinary things of life are viewed as extraordinary and in which the daily sufferings and pettiness are offered to God. She also compared herself to a "little flower" or to a child. "I behave like children who cannot read: I tell God very simply what I want and he understands." The following quotation is from* The Story of a Soul:

> How happy I am to realize that I am little and weak, how happy I am to see myself so imperfect. It is needful to remain little before God and to remain little is to recognize one's nothingness, expect all things from the good God just as a little child expects all things from its father; it is not to be troubled by any-thing, not to try to make a fortune. Even

among poor people, a child is given all it needs, as long as it is very little, but as soon as it has grown up, the father does not want to support it any longer and says: "Work, now you are able to take care of yourself." Because I never want to hear these words I do not want to grow up, feeling that I can never earn my living, that is, eternal life in heaven. So I have stayed little, and have no other occupation than of gathering flowers of love and sacrifice and of offering them to the good God to please Him.

For a long time I had been asking myself why souls did not all receive the same amount of grace. Jesus deigned to instruct me about this mystery. Before my eyes He placed the book of nature and I understood that all the flowers created by Him are beautiful . . . that, if all the little flowers wanted to be roses, nature would lose her springtime garb. The same is true of the world of souls, the Lord's living garden. God's love is revealed just as much in the most simple soul who does not resist His graces as in the most sublime.

Personal Conversation with Jesus

- Ask Jesus to tell you why he loves you. What did he say?

- How can you keep the innocence of a child?

- Recognize all things as little things (except securing your salvation and the salvation of others). Ask Jesus how to do this.

Lumen Gentium: *The Foundation of the Church Is Announced in Sacred Scripture*

The Dogmatic Constitution on the Church Lumen Gentium *(The Light of Nations), perhaps the most important document of the Second Vatican Council, updated the Church's self-image by emphasizing the mystery of the Church as a community, as the People of God, and as a sacrament or sign of God's presence in the world.* Lumen Gentium *also reminds Catholics that everyone in the Church—clergy and laity alike—is called to holiness, and it stresses the collegiality between the pope and bishops. In the following quotation from paragraph 5, the document traces the mystery of the Church to its very beginnings, which are spoken by Jesus and recorded in sacred scripture.*

> The mystery of the holy Church is manifest in its very foundation. The Lord Jesus set it on its course by preaching the Good News, that is, the coming of the Kingdom of God, which, for centuries, had been promised in the Scriptures: "The time is fulfilled, and the kingdom of God is at hand." In the word, in the works, and in the presence of Christ, this kingdom was clearly open to the view of men. The Word of the Lord is compared to a seed which is sown in

a field; those who hear the Word with faith and become part of the little flock of Christ, have received the Kingdom itself. Then, by its own power the seed sprouts and grows until harvest time. The Miracles of Jesus also confirm that the Kingdom has already arrived on earth: "If I cast out devils by the finger of God, then the kingdom of God has come upon you." Before all things, however, the Kingdom is clearly visible in the very Person of Christ, the Son of God and the Son of Man, who came "to serve and to give His life as a ransom for many."

When Jesus, who had suffered the death of the cross for mankind, had risen, He appeared as the one constituted as Lord, Christ and eternal Priest, and He poured out on His disciples the Spirit promised by the Father. From this source the Church, equipped with the gifts of its Founder and faithfully guarding His precepts of charity, humility and self-sacrifice, receives the mission to proclaim and to spread among all peoples the Kingdom of Christ and of God and to be, on earth, the initial budding forth of that kingdom. While it slowly grows, the Church strains toward the completed Kingdom and, with all its strength, hopes and desires to be united in glory with its King.

Personal Conversation with Jesus

- Ask Jesus: How is the kingdom of God at hand?

- Meditate on a miracle of Jesus. What does it reveal about him?

- How can you share the kingdom of God with others?

Spiritus Paraclitus:
Sacred Scripture Is Christ's Teaching

Spiritus Paraclitus *(The Spirit, the Comforter), an encyclical by Pope Benedict XV published in 1920 on the 1,500th anniversary of the death of St. Jerome, also came at a time when Catholic biblical scholars were questioning the historicity of the Bible. Pope Benedict countered the arguments and promoted study and reading of the Bible in the spirit of St. Jerome's commentary. The encyclical summarizes the doctrines of inerrancy and inspiration of sacred scripture. In paragraphs 28–30 we read:*

> Neither Jerome nor the other Fathers of the Church learned their doctrine touching Holy Scripture save in the school of the Divine Master Himself. We know what He felt about Holy Scripture: when He said, "It is written," and "the Scripture must needs be fulfilled," we have therein an argument which admits of no exception and which should put an end to all controversy.

> Yet it is worthwhile dwelling on this point a little: when Christ preached to the people, whether on the Mount by the lakeside, or in the synagogue at Nazareth, or in His own city of

Capharnaum, He took His points and His arguments from the Bible. From the same source came His weapons when disputing with the Scribes and Pharisees. Whether teaching or disputing He quotes from all parts of Scripture and takes His example from it; He quotes it as an argument which must be accepted. He refers without any discrimination of sources to the stories of [Jonah] and the Ninivites, of the Queen of Sheba and Solomon, of [Elijah] and [Elisha], of David and of [Noah], of Lot and the Sodomites, and even of Lot's wife (cf. Mt 12:3, 39–42; Lk 17:26–29, 32). How solemn His witness to the truth of the sacred books: "One jot, or one tittle shall not pass of the Law till all be fulfilled" (Mt 5:18); and again: "The Scripture cannot be broken" (Jn 10:35); and consequently: "He therefore that shall break one of these least commandments, and shall so teach men shall be called the least in the kingdom of heaven" (Mt. 5:19). Before His Ascension, too, when He would steep His Apostles in the same doctrine: "He opened their understanding that they might understand the Scriptures. And He said to them: thus it is written, and thus it [behooved] Christ to suffer, and to rise again from the dead the third day" (Lk 24:45).

In a word, then: Jerome's teaching on the superexcellence and truth of Scripture is Christ's teaching.

Personal Conversation with Jesus

- Recall something Jesus said in scripture with the understanding that these are the words from the mouth of God.

- What was last Sunday's Gospel reading? How does it speak directly to you?

- "Scripture is Christ's teaching." What does Jesus wish to teach you today?

Dei Verbum:
Sacred Scripture in the Life of the Church

The Second Vatican Council document Dei Verbum *(The Word of God) is a commentary on divine revelation in the life of the Church, including encouragement for all people—clergy and laity—to take up prayer, reading, and study of the Bible. The document also addresses the relationship between sacred scripture and sacred tradition. The Church's Deposit of Faith consists of both sacred scripture and sacred tradition. Both flow from the same source (God) and have the same goal (human salvation through Jesus Christ). Further, as paragraph 21 of* Dei Verbum *emphasizes, sacred scripture, as the Word of God, is equated with Christ himself. The words of the Bible are spoken from the very lips of God.*

> The Church has always venerated the divine Scriptures just as she venerates the body of the Lord, since, especially in the sacred liturgy, she unceasingly receives and offers to the faithful the bread of life from the table both of God's word and of Christ's body. She has always maintained them, and continues to do so, together with sacred tradition, as the supreme rule of faith, since, as inspired by God and

committed once and for all to writing, they impart the word of God Himself without change, and make the voice of the Holy Spirit resound in the words of the prophets and Apostles. Therefore, like the Christian religion itself, all the preaching of the Church must be nourished and regulated by Sacred Scripture. For in the sacred books, the Father who is in heaven meets His children with great love and speaks with them; and the force and power in the word of God is so great that it stands as the support and energy of the Church, the strength of faith for her sons, the food of the soul, the pure and everlasting source of spiritual life. Consequently these words are perfectly applicable to Sacred Scripture: "For the word of God is living and active" (Heb 4:12) and "it has power to build you up and give you your heritage among all those who are sanctified" (Acts 20:32; see 1 Thes 2:13).

Personal Conversation with Jesus

- Think about a family or personal Bible you have in your home. Why is it significant to you?

- Tell Jesus about a goal you have for increased praying, reading, and studying the Bible.

- How do you understand the statement "For the word of God is living and active"?

General Instruction of the Roman Missal: The Liturgy of the Word

In 2002, St. John Paul II introduced a new edition of the Roman Missal, which is the book that contains the prayers, chants, and other instructions for the celebration of the Mass in the Roman Catholic Church. In 2011, the Church in the United States began to use a new English edition of the Roman Missal. Soon after, the United States Conference of Catholic Bishops introduced the General Instruction of the Roman Missal. These two documents provide a comprehensive overview and instruction for the celebration of Mass for both clergy and laity. The following text is from the Liturgy of the Word subsection (paragraphs 55–57, 60).

The main part of the Liturgy of the Word is made up of the readings from Sacred Scripture together with the chants occurring between them. As for the Homily, the Profession of Faith, and the Universal Prayer, they develop and conclude it. For in the readings, as explained by the Homily, God speaks to his people, opening up to them the mystery of redemption and salvation, and offering spiritual nourishment; and Christ himself is present through his word in the midst of the faithful. By silence and by singing, the people make this divine word their own, and affirm their adherence to it by means of the Profession of Faith; finally, having been nourished by the divine word, the people pour out their petitions by means of the Universal Prayer for the needs of the whole Church and for the salvation of the whole world.

The Liturgy of the Word is to be celebrated in such a way as to favor meditation, and so any kind of haste such as hinders recollection is clearly to be avoided. In the course of it, brief periods of silence are also appropriate, accommodated to the assembled congregation; by means of these, under the action of the Holy Spirit, the Word of God may be grasped by the heart and a response through prayer may be prepared. . . .

The reading of the Gospel constitutes the high point of the Liturgy of the Word. The Liturgy itself teaches the great reverence that is to be shown to this reading by setting it off from the other readings with special marks of honor, by the fact of which minister is appointed to proclaim it and by the blessing or prayer with which he prepares himself; and also by the fact that through their acclamations the faithful acknowledge and confess that Christ is present and is speaking to them and stand as they listen to the reading; and by the mere fact of the marks of reverence that are given to the Book of the Gospels.

Personal Conversation with Jesus

- Explore the connection between the Old Testament reading and the gospel from a Mass you most recently attended.

- What does it mean to you to show reverence for God's Word?

- Repeat the mantra "Praise to you, Lord Jesus Christ."

Adoration and Sacrifice

The Mass is a true and proper sacrifice that is offered to God. It is indeed identical with Christ's one sacrifice, re-presented in an unbloody way. The same Jesus on Calvary, now glorified, is present on the altar. It was impossible, as the Letter to the Hebrews states, "that the blood of bulls and goats take away sins" (Heb 10:4). Jesus's Body was prepared to be the one and only sacrifice and offering. At Mass, Christ re-presents the sacrifice he made at Calvary. They are one and the same thing. It is appropriate and necessary to meditate often on Christ's sacrificial offering. In Eucharistic Adoration, with Christ truly in our presence, we remember God's most miraculous gift, the gift of his only begotten Son.

Anima Christi

For many years the Anima Christi (Soul of Christ) was attributed to the authorship of St. Ignatius Loyola, the founder of the Jesuits in the sixteenth century. However, the origins of the prayer are actually two centuries earlier. St. Ignatius did feature the Anima Christi in his classic Spiritual Exercises. This prayer is a meditation on Christ's Passion and a hopeful petition for eternal life. The line about "water from the side of Christ" refers to when the Roman soldier thrust his lance into Christ's side when he was on the Cross and "blood and water flowed out" (Jn 19:34).

Soul of Christ, sanctify me.
Body of Christ, save me.
Blood of Christ, inebriate me.
Water from the side of Christ, wash me.
Passion of Christ, strengthen me.
O good Jesus, hear me.
Within your wounds conceal me.
Do not permit me to be parted from
    you.
From the evil foe protect me.
At the hour of my death call me.
And bid me come to you,
to praise you with all your saints
for ever and ever.
Amen.

Personal Conversation with Jesus

- Repeat one or more of the petitions in the prayer as a mantra.

- Picture yourself on Calvary at the foot of the Cross. Say something to Jesus.

- How can you offer yourself for others in Jesus's name?

Litany of the Sacred Heart of Jesus

Devotion to the Sacred Heart of Jesus has long been a tradition in the Church. Understanding that the beating heart that began in the womb of Mary continues to pour out mercy and love on the world leads to contemplation on this great gift. In the seventeenth century, St. Margaret Mary Alacoque received visions from Christ telling her she should spread devotion to his Sacred Heart. In 1899, Pope Leo XIII approved the Litany of the Sacred Heart of Jesus for the entire Church. The litany is made up of petitions from three different sources. A partial indulgence is attached to praying the litany.

Lord, have mercy
Lord, have mercy
Christ, have mercy
Christ, have mercy
Lord, have mercy
Lord, have mercy

God our Father in heaven
have mercy on us
God the Son, Redeemer of the world
have mercy on us
God the Holy Spirit
have mercy on us
Holy Trinity, one God
have mercy on us

Heart of Jesus, Son of the eternal Father
have mercy on us
Heart of Jesus, formed by the Holy Spirit
 in the womb of the Virgin Mother
have mercy on us
Heart of Jesus, one with the eternal Word
have mercy on us
Heart of Jesus, infinite in majesty
have mercy on us
Heart of Jesus, holy temple of God
have mercy on us
Heart of Jesus, tabernacle of the Most High
have mercy on us

Heart of Jesus, house of God and gate
 of heaven
have mercy on us
Heart of Jesus, aflame with love for us
have mercy on us
Heart of Jesus, source of justice and love
have mercy on us
Heart of Jesus, full of goodness and love
have mercy on us
Heart of Jesus, well-spring of all virtue
have mercy on us
Heart of Jesus, worthy of all praise
have mercy on us

Heart of Jesus, king and center of all hearts

have mercy on us

Heart of Jesus, treasure-house of wisdom and knowledge

have mercy on us

Heart of Jesus, in whom there dwells the fullness of God

have mercy on us

Heart of Jesus, in whom the Father is well pleased

have mercy on us

Heart of Jesus, from whose fullness we have all received

have mercy on us

Heart of Jesus, desire of the eternal hills

have mercy on us

Heart of Jesus, patient and full of mercy

have mercy on us

Heart of Jesus, generous to all who turn to you

have mercy on us

Heart of Jesus, fountain of life and holiness

have mercy on us

Heart of Jesus, atonement for our sins

have mercy on us

Heart of Jesus, overwhelmed with insults

have mercy on us

Heart of Jesus, broken for our sins

have mercy on us

Heart of Jesus, obedient even to death

have mercy on us

Heart of Jesus, pierced by a lance

have mercy on us

Heart of Jesus, source of all consolation

have mercy on us

Heart of Jesus, our life and resurrection

have mercy on us

Heart of Jesus, our peace and reconciliation

have mercy on us

Heart of Jesus, victim of our sins

have mercy on us

Heart of Jesus, salvation of all who trust in you

have mercy on us

Heart of Jesus, hope of all who die in you

have mercy on us

Heart of Jesus, delight of all the saints

have mercy on us

Lamb of God, you take away the sins of the world

have mercy on us

Lamb of God, you take away the sins
of the world
have mercy on us
Lamb of God, you take away the sins
of the world
have mercy on us
Jesus, gentle and humble of heart.
Touch our hearts and make them like your own.

Let us pray.
Grant, we pray, almighty God,
that we, who glory in the Heart of your
beloved Son
and recall the wonders of his love for us,
may be made worthy to receive
an overflowing measure of grace
from that fount of heavenly gifts.
Through Christ our Lord.
Amen.

Personal Conversation with Jesus

- Offer your prayer for someone in need of God's love.

- Imagine the endless love that flows from the Sacred
  Heart of Jesus.

- Which line of the novena stands out the most for
  you?

The Rosary of the Seven Sorrows

The Rosary of the Seven Sorrows is a unique form of the Rosary that allows us to accompany Mary through seven experiences of sorrow and suffering that are described in the gospels. The prayer has origins in the fourteenth century when Mary, under the title of Our Lady of Sorrows, appeared to St. Bridget of Sweden and revealed this devotion to her. The Rosary begins with the Sign of the Cross, three Hail Marys, and the Most Merciful Mother petition (see below). For the seven mysteries, begin by naming and reading each account from the gospels. Repeat at each mystery one Our Father, seven Hail Marys, and one Most Merciful Mother. The seven mysteries are (1) The Prophecy of Simeon (Lk 2:34–35); (2) The Flight into Egypt (Mt 2:13–14); (3) The Loss of Jesus in the Temple (Lk 2:43–45); (4) Mary Meets Jesus on the Way to Calvary (Lk 23:27–29); (5) Mary Stands at the Foot of the Cross (Jn 19:25–27); (6) Jesus Is Taken Down from the Cross (Jn 19:32–34); and (7) The Burial of Jesus (Jn 19:41–42). After all seven mysteries, pray the closing prayer three times (see below).

> *Pray once after the three opening Hail Marys, and at the conclusion of each mystery:*
>
> Most Merciful Mother, remind us always about the Sorrow of your Son, Jesus.
>
> *Pray the closing prayer three times:*
>
> Mary, who was conceived without sin and who suffered for us, pray for us.

Personal Conversation with Jesus

- How did understanding Jesus's suffering through the eyes of Mary enlighten you?

- Think about how Jesus felt as he witnessed the suffering of his Mother.

- Repeat this mantra: "Pray for us, O Virgin most sorrowful, that we may be worthy of the promises of Christ."

The Mystery of Faith

The words "The Mystery of Faith" that are recited by the priest at the end of the consecration during the Eucharistic Prayers were originally placed within the Rite of Consecration of the chalice and spoken by the priest: "For this is the Chalice of my Blood, of the new and eternal Covenant: the Mystery of Faith: which shall be shed for you and for many unto the remission of sins." When new Eucharistic Prayers were introduced after the Second Vatican Council, several debates and revisions took place before Pope St. Paul VI mandated that the expression "Mysterium fidei" be used in all Eucharistic Prayers in the form of dialogue between the priest and people. The priest says, "The Mystery of Faith," and the people respond with one of the three acclamations listed below. The meaning of "The Mystery of Faith" is associated first with the miracle of the ordinary bread and wine being changed into the Body and Blood of Christ. The "mystery" also refers to the mystery of Christ's entire life, that God's own Son would enter the world in human form to offer himself for our redemption.

> We proclaim your Death, O Lord, and profess your Resurrection until you come again.

> When we eat this Bread and drink this Cup, we proclaim your Death, O Lord, until you come again.

Save us, Savior of the world, for by your Cross and Resurrection you have set us free.

Personal Conversation with Jesus

- Repeat one or more of these acclamations as a mantra.

- How do you proclaim the Death of the Lord, Jesus Christ?

- Reflect on the mystery of transubstantiation that occurs at Mass.

Deuteronomy 8:2-3

As the Israelites journeyed for forty years in the desert, they learned several times over that everything in this life is a gift from God. Even the sufferings and sacrifices they endured were in preparation for their ultimate goal of reaching the Promised Land. Another lesson was that they learned which gifts from God were truly the important ones. The bread that fed their bodies was not as important as God's Word, which fed their souls.

Remember how for these forty years the LORD, your God, has directed all your journeying in the wilderness, so as to test you by affliction to know what was in your heart: to keep his commandments, or not. He therefore let you be afflicted with hunger, and then fed you with manna, a food unknown to you and your ancestors, so you might know that it is not by bread alone that people live, but by all that comes forth from the mouth of the LORD.

Personal Conversation with Jesus

- How do you recognize everything in your life as a gift from God?

- How do your sufferings and sacrifices make you stronger?

- How is Jesus the food that sustains you?

Psalm 145:10-11, 15-18

Psalm 145 is a hymn written in acrostic form; that is, every letter of each verse begins with a successive letter of the Hebrew alphabet. The message itself is about the greatness and goodness of God. His mighty acts show his kingship over us and our dependence on him for all of our needs.

> All your works give you thanks, LORD
>> and your faithful bless you.
> They speak of the glory of your reign
>> and tell of your mighty works. . . .
> The eyes of all look hopefully to you;
>> you give them their food in due season.
> You open wide your hand
>> and satisfy the desire of every living thing.
> The LORD is just in all his ways,
>> merciful in his works.
> The LORD is near to all who call upon him,
>> to all who call upon him in truth.

Personal Conversation with Jesus

- Pray in your own words a prayer of praise for God's glory.

- Pray in your own words a prayer of thanksgiving for God's blessings to you.

- Jesus is with you now. Bare your soul to him in truth.

1 Corinthians 11:23-26

This earliest written account of the institution of the Eucharist in the New Testament points to Jesus's offering of his entire self, made present in the blessed bread and wine. The Catechism of the Catholic Church *reminds us that the "Eucharistic presence of Christ begins at the moment of consecration and endures as long as the Eucharistic species subsist" (1377).*

> For I received from the Lord what I also handed on to you, that the Lord Jesus, on the night he was handed over, took bread, and, after he had given thanks, broke it and said, "This is my body that is for you. Do this in remembrance of me." In the same way also the cup, after supper, saying, "This cup is the new covenant in my blood. Do this, as often as you drink it, in remembrance of me." For as often as you eat this bread and drink the cup, you proclaim the death of the Lord until he comes.

Personal Conversation with Jesus

- Reflect on the meaning of "Real Presence."

- Imagine yourself at the Last Supper, at the moment when Jesus speaks these words.

- How can you better prepare yourself to be attentive at Mass? Bring this question to Jesus.

John 6:35, 53-54

In conjunction with Jesus's sign of the multiplication of loaves, the Gospel of John presents Jesus's teaching about his identity as the "bread of life." Speaking in a Capernaum synagogue, Jesus says that he replaces the manna of the Exodus. He is the new bread God has given to his disciples. Through Jesus, all his followers will pass over from death to new life.

> I am the bread of life; whoever comes to me will never hunger, and whoever believes in me will never thirst. . . . Amen, amen, I say to you, unless you eat the flesh of the Son of Man and drink his blood, you do not have life within you. Whoever eats my flesh and drinks my blood has eternal life, and I will raise him on the last day.

Personal Conversation with Jesus

- Read the passage a second and third time. Which words especially stand out?

- Many of Jesus's first disciples found these words difficult. Share your reaction to them with Jesus as if you heard them for the first time.

- Compose a one-line prayer in your own words that you can say to yourself after receiving Holy Communion.

St. Maximilian Kolbe: The Crown of Suffering

At age twelve, in 1906, Raymond Kolbe had a vision of the Blessed Virgin Mary. Her message prepared him for the future. Later, as a priest, Fr. Maximilian recalled the vision: "I asked the Mother of God what was to become of me. Then she came to me holding two crowns, one white, the other red. She asked if I was willing to accept either of these crowns. The white one meant that I should persevere in purity, the red that I should become a martyr. I said that I would accept them both." Arrested during World War II for opposing the Nazis when they invaded his native Poland, St. Maximilian Kolbe was sentenced to Auschwitz. When a prisoner escaped the prison, a group of ten was selected for death by starvation as a lesson to the other prisoners. Among the group was a Jewish man who pleaded to be spared. St. Maximilian stepped forward and said, "I am a Catholic priest. Let me take his place. I am old. He has a wife and children." The Nazis agreed. The prisoners were locked into a bunker with no food or drink. St. Maximillian prayed the Rosary, sang hymns to Mary, and taught others about Jesus. After two weeks, St. Maximillian was the only prisoner still alive. He was then killed with a lethal injection of carbolic acid. He had accepted both crowns, the white of purity and the red of martyrdom. He had also left the world with a memorable example of how love and sacrifice are intertwined.

Let us remember that love lives through
sacrifice and is nourished by giving. Let's
remember that not everything which is

good and beautiful pertains to genuine, essential love, because even without those other things love can be present, indeed a perfected love. Without sacrifice there is no love. Sacrifice the senses, taste, hearing, and above all, the mind and the will in holy obedience. I wish for you and for myself the best appreciation of sacrifice which is the unconditional willingness to sacrifice.

Personal Conversation with Jesus

- "Without sacrifice there is no love." Reflect on these words in relation to Christ's Passion and Death.

- How have you found love in sacrifice?

- Tell Jesus about your willingness to give up everything for him.

St. Teresa of Calcutta:
Suffering Is the Kiss of Jesus

In 1950, Mother Teresa founded the Missionaries of Charity in Calcutta. The apostolate, or mission, of this religious community, she explained, was to care "for people who have become a burden to society and are shunned by everyone." By the time of her death in 1997, the Missionaries of Charity had grown to four thousand sisters, three hundred brothers, and more than one hundred thousand laypeople. St. Teresa of Calcutta was canonized by Pope Francis on September 4, 2016. She reminds us of the value of suffering.

Suffering—pain, humiliation, sickness, and failure—is but a kiss of Jesus.

Once I met a lady who had a terrible cancer. She was suffering so much. I told her, "Now you come so close to Jesus on the cross that he is kissing you." Then she joined hands and said, "Mother Teresa, please tell Jesus to stop kissing me." It was so beautiful. She understood.

Suffering is a gift of God that makes us most Christ-like. People must not accept suffering as punishment.

At Christmas I was talking to our lepers and telling them that the leprosy is a gift from God. I told them that God can trust them so much and that he gives them this terrible suffering. These lepers were lonely, like Jesus when he came to earth. Jesus was also very lonely because as a human being he was away from the Father.

And one man who was completely disfigured started pulling at my sari. "Repeat that," he said. "Repeat that our suffering is God's love. Those who are suffering understand you when you talk like this, Mother Teresa."

Christ is really living his passion in our lepers. In our people you can see Calvary.

Personal Conversation with Jesus

- Jesus tells you he is going to give you a kiss of suffering. What do you say to him?

- Pray with Jesus for someone you know who is suffering.

- Tell Jesus about your own suffering. Offer it to him.

St. Francis of Assisi:
Be Worthy in Reception of the Eucharist

Seventeen letters are attributed to St. Francis of Assisi. In Letter XIII, addressed to clerics (Francis was not ordained), he laments against a lackadaisical and disrespectful treatment of the way the Sacred Body and Blood of Christ are displayed in churches and chapels, as well as the unworthy distribution and reception of Holy Communion by priests and the faithful. As Catholics, we never should "go through the motions" when it comes to Jesus's Real Presence in the Eucharist. It is sacred for us to genuflect in respect when we pass before the tabernacle. More importantly, we must receive Holy Communion worthily. This means, as canon law states, anyone "conscious of grave sin" should not "receive the body of the Lord without previous sacramental confession" (916). Read St. Francis's letter to the clerics with attention to your own respect and reverence for the Body and Blood of Christ present in the Eucharist.

To All Clerics,

To my Reverend Masters, all the clerics of the whole world, who live according to the rules of the Catholic Faith, little Brother Francis, their least servant, greeting, with all possible reverence, and humbly kissing their feet. Since I am become a debtor to all, but cannot now, on account of my infirmities, address you personally, I implore you to receive with all love and charity this admonition and instruction, which I write to you in few words. Consider, O clerics, the great sin and ignorance of which some are guilty towards the Sacred Body and Blood of Our Lord Jesus Christ, His holy Name, and written Words, by which His Body is consecrated; for we know that the Body of Jesus Christ is not present until His Sacred Words are pronounced. We have nothing, and can see nothing corporally of God in this world, except the Body and Blood of Jesus Christ, His holy Name and Words, by which we were created, and by which we have been restored from death to life. Let all those who minister in these most holy Mysteries, and especially those who do so carelessly, consider well within themselves whether the chalices, corporals, and linen which are used in the most adorable Sacrifice of the Body and Blood of Christ, be in a becoming state; whether Our Lord is not left in an improper place, carried about disrespectfully, received unworthily, and indiscreetly given to others. Sometimes even His holy Name and His written Word are trampled underfoot, for the animal man cannot understand the things of God. Shall we not be moved to grief by this when we consider that this sweet Lord places Himself in our hands, and that we daily touch Him and receive Him in our mouth? Do we not know that one day we shall fall into His Hands? Let us then at once courageously correct ourselves of these faults and others; and wherever we find the Sacred Body of Our Lord kept disrespectfully and neglected, let us remove It thence, and securely place It in a carefully prepared tabernacle. And in like manner, if we find the Name or the written Words of Our Lord in unclean places, let us at once collect them, and put them away respectfully. And let us remember that we are bound to observe these things by the commandments of God, and the constitutions of our holy Mother the Church. And let him who neglects this know that he will have to give an account thereof before Our Lord Jesus Christ in the day of judgment. That this writing may be the better observed, let those be blessed by God who cause copies to be made of it. May Our Lord Jesus Christ fill you all, my Masters, with His grace and strength. Amen.

Personal Conversation with Jesus

- Confess your unworthiness to receive Jesus in Holy Communion. Make plans to go to Confession as soon as possible.

- Observe the surroundings and place of honor for the Blessed Sacrament where you are.

- Tell Jesus more about your own suffering. Offer it to him.

St. Teresa of Ávila: No Other Joy

St. Teresa of Ávila was a Church reformer and a mystic who lived following the Protestant Reformation. Her Interior Castle *is a spiritual classic that outlines the various steps of contemplative prayer. She is also known as a "Eucharistic saint"; she had great devotion for the Lord in the Blessed Sacrament. Through regular prayer and penance, she deepened her spiritual life and received spiritual ecstasies: a trance of joy and delight in the Lord. In this verse she shares the desire she feels for the Eucharist from the time the priest unlocks the tabernacle until the blessed host reaches her lips.*

> Little Key, oh, I envy you!
> For each day you can open
> The prison of the Eucharist
> Where the God of Love resides.
> But, O what a sweet miracle!
> By just an effort of my faith
> I can also open the tabernacle
> To hide near the Divine King. . . .
>
> Being consumed near my God
> In the sanctuary,
> I would like to burn forever with mystery
> Like the Lamp of the Holy Place. . . .
> Oh! what happiness . . . I have flames
>   within me,

And each day I can win
A great number of souls for Jesus,

Inflaming them with his love. . . .
At each daybreak I envy you,
O Sacred Altar Stone! As in the blessed
stable,
On you the Eternal One wants to be
born. . . .
Ah! Deign to grant my prayer.
Come into my soul, Sweet Savior. . . .
Far from being a cold stone,
It is the sigh of your Heart!

O Corporal surrounded by angels!
How enviable is your lot.
On you, as in his humble swaddling
clothes,
I see Jesus, my only treasure.
Virgin Mary, change my heart
Into a pure, beautiful Corporal
To receive the white host,
Where your Sweet Lamb hides.

Holy Paten, I envy you.
Upon you Jesus comes to rest.
Oh! may his infinite grandeur

Deign to humble itself even to me. . . .
Fulfilling my hope, Jesus
Does not wait until the evening of my
    life.
He comes within me; by his presence
I am a living Monstrance! . . .

Oh! how I envy the happy chalice
Where I adore the divine Blood. . . .
But at the Holy Sacrifice
I can take it in each morning.
To Jesus my soul is dearer
Than precious vessels of gold.
The Altar is a new Calvary
Where his Blood still flows for me. . . .

Jesus, holy and sacred Vine,
O my Divine King,
You know I am a cluster of golden
    grapes
Which must disappear for you.
Under the wine press of suffering,
I shall prove my love for you.
I want no other joy
Than to sacrifice myself each day.

Ah! what joy, I am chosen

Among the grains of pure Wheat
Who lose their lives for Jesus.
My delight is truly great! . . .
I am your dear spouse,
My Beloved, come live in me,
Oh! come, your beauty has ravished me.
Deign to transform me into You!

Personal Conversation with Jesus

- Imagine the eternal God contained in the tabernacle that sits before you.

- Recite the verse a second time. Imagine each step in the progression from the locked tabernacle to its place on your tongue at Communion.

- Compose your own two-line prayer verse to Jesus, thanking him for the gift of his Body and Blood.

Council of Trent: Christ's Everlasting Gift

Christ continues to offer the same Body and Blood he offered at his death on Calvary. He does this in order to apply the fruits gained by his death to people of every age. The Council of Trent (quoted in the Catechism of the Catholic Church, *1366) states:*

> [Christ], our Lord and God, was once and for all to offer himself to God the Father by his death on the altar of the cross, to accomplish there an everlasting redemption. But because his priesthood was not to end with his death, at the Last Supper "on the night when he was betrayed," [he wanted] to leave to his beloved spouse the Church a visible sacrifice (as the nature of man demands) by which the bloody sacrifice which he was to accomplish once for all on the cross would be re-presented, its memory perpetuated until the end of the world, and its salutary power be applied to the forgiveness of the sins we daily commit.

Personal Conversation with Jesus

- Explore in meditation the heavenly banquet. What will it be like? Who will be there?

- How can you sense that death holds no power over you?

- Absorb yourself in your forgiven sins.

Didache:
Be Prepared for the Coming of the Lord

The catechetical document the Didache *(Teaching) was written perhaps as early as AD 60 but more likely around 100. The author is unknown. The* Didache *mentions the Trinitarian formula, lists moral teachings, and explains the rites of Baptism and Eucharist. It highlights that the Eucharist forms Christians into a new people: "Even as this bread was scattered over the hills, and was gathered together becoming one, so let your Church be gathered together from the ends of the earth into your kingdom" (9). Chapter 14 reminds Christians to prepare themselves well for the Eucharist so that their sacrifice may be pure. Chapter 16 (below) concludes the* Didache *by instructing Christians to prepare for Christ's Second Coming.*

Watch for your life's sake. Let not your lamps be quenched, nor your loins unloosed; but be ready, for you know not the hour in which our Lord will come. But come together often, seeking the things which are befitting to your souls: for the whole time of your faith will not profit you, if you are not made perfect in the last time. For in the last days false prophets and corrupters shall be multiplied, and the sheep shall be turned into wolves, and love shall be turned into hate; for when lawlessness increases, they shall hate and persecute and betray one another, and then shall appear the world-deceiver as Son of God, and shall do signs and wonders, and the earth shall be delivered into his hands, and he shall do iniquitous things which have never yet come to pass since the beginning. Then shall the creation of men come into the fire of trial, and many shall be made to stumble and shall perish; but they that endure in their faith shall be saved from under the curse itself. And then shall appear the signs of the truth; first, the sign of an outspreading in heaven; then the sign of the sound of the trumpet; and the third, the resurrection of the dead; yet not of all, but as it is said: "The Lord shall come and all His saints with Him." Then shall the world see the Lord coming upon the clouds of heaven.

Personal Conversation with Jesus

- Ask the Lord to keep you company on your watch at all times.

- Share a prayer asking Christ's protection from evil. Name specific evils.

- Create your own vision of the Lord's Second Coming.

Ecclesia de Eucharista: *A Sacrificial Gift to the Father and the Church*

Ecclesia de Eucharista *(*The Church Draws Her Life from the Eucharist*) is an encyclical by St. John Paul II written in 2003. His purpose was to remind the Church of the centrality of the Mass to the purpose and mission of the lives of all Catholics. He emphasized that the Mass always makes present the sacrifice of Christ on the Cross. While a gift for us, the sacrificial offering was primarily a mutual gift to the Father, who had preordained his Son from all time to save the world from sin. By completing his mission, Jesus offered this gift back to him. This point is made in paragraph 13:*

> By virtue of its close relationship to the sacrifice of Golgotha, the Eucharist *is a sacrifice in the strict sense*, and not only in a general way, as if it were simply a matter of Christ's offering himself to the faithful as their spiritual food. The gift of his love and obedience to the point of giving his life (cf. Jn 10:17–18) is in the first place a gift to his Father. Certainly it is a gift given for our sake, and indeed that of all humanity (cf. Mt 26:28; Mk 14:24; Lk 22:20; Jn 10:15), yet it is *first and foremost a gift to the Father*:

"a sacrifice that the Father accepted, giving, in return for this total self-giving by his Son, who 'became obedient unto death' (Phil 2:8), his own paternal gift, that is to say the grant of new immortal life in the resurrection."

In giving his sacrifice to the Church, Christ has also made his own the spiritual sacrifice of the Church, which is called to offer herself in union with the sacrifice of Christ. This is the teaching of the Second Vatican Council concerning all the faithful: "Taking part in the Eucharistic Sacrifice, which is the source and summit of the whole Christian life, they offer the divine victim to God, and offer themselves along with it."

Personal Conversation with Jesus

- Delve into the love between Jesus and the Father.

- Think about how you have been the recipient of gifts from your family members and how you have gifted them in return.

- Ponder the love God the Father has for you as his unique creation.

Homilies on First Corinthians:
A Communion in the Blood of Christ

St. John Chrysostom was a post–Nicene Council Church Father. He was nicknamed "Golden Mouth" because of his skills as a preacher. As bishop in Constantinople, he preached against the moral laxity of civil leaders, which resulted in his being exiled twice. He died during the second exile in AD 407. In this selection from Homilies on First Corinthians *(24), he preaches on St. Paul's words that the wine consecrated into Christ's Blood at Mass makes animal sacrifice obsolete. Christ's own sacrifice of his Body and Blood is a blessing poured out for all.*

"The cup of blessing which we bless, is it not communion of the blood of Christ?" Very trustworthy and awesomely does he [Paul] say it. For what he is saying is this: What is in the cup is that which flowed from his side, and we partake of it. He called it a cup of blessing because when we hold it in our hands that is how we praise him in song, wondering and astonished at his indescribable gift, blessing him because of his having poured out this very gift so that we might not remain in error; and not only for his having poured it out, but also for his sharing it with all of us. "If therefore you desire blood," he [the Lord] says, "do not redden the platform of idols with the slaughter of dumb beasts, but my altar of sacrifice with my blood." What is more awesome than this? What, pray tell, more tenderly loving?

In ancient times, because men were very imperfect, God did not scorn to receive the blood which they were offering . . . to draw them away from those idols; and this very thing again was because of his indescribable, tender affection. But now he has transferred the priestly action to what is most awesome and magnificent. He has changed the sacrifice itself, and instead of the butchering of dumb beasts, he commands the offering up of himself.

Personal Conversation with Jesus

- Thank Jesus for the blessings that poured forth from his side.

- Reflect on the "awesome" and "loving" nature of Christ's sacrifice.

- Pray for someone you know to come to a relationship with Jesus.

The Ave Guide to Eucharistic Adoration

Adoration and Service

The Mass seems to end abruptly with the Concluding Rites. There is a Prayer after Communion, and then through the ministry of the priest, God blesses the people: "May almighty God bless you, the Father, and the Son, and the Holy Spirit." After the blessing, we are dismissed. In fact, the Mass does not end. We are sent out to fulfill the Church's mission. The word "Mass" comes from the Latin word *missa*, which means "sent." "Mass" also has origins in the word *missio* or "mission." Just as Jesus commissioned and sent his apostles to teach the entire world about him and his message (see Mt 28:19–20), so the Church sends you forth from the Eucharist to share your communion with the Blessed Trinity, with the Church, and with the world at large, especially the poor by satisfying their needs. The sanctifying grace of the Eucharist empowers you to go forth and to be Eucharist for others.

Prayer for Vocations

The word "vocation" has roots in the Latin word vocatio, *which means "call" or "summons." By our Baptism, we are all called to a common Christian vocation to live a life in Christ and to evangelize the world with our words and actions. There are specific vocations within our baptismal vocation—for example, to the priesthood (for males), to the consecrated life, and to marriage. The following prayer from the United States Conference of Catholic Bishops is intended as a prayer for an increase in ministry vocations in the Church.*

Father, we're your people, the work of
    your hands.
So precious are we in your sight that you
    sent your Son, Jesus.
Jesus calls us to heal the broken-hearted,
to dry the tears of those who mourn, to
    give hope to those who despair,
and to rejoice in your steadfast love.
We, the baptized, realize our call to
    serve.
Help us to know how.
Call forth from among us priests, sisters,
    brothers and lay ministers.
With our hearts you continue to love
    your people.

We ask this through our Lord Jesus
Christ, your Son,
who lives and reigns with you and the
Holy Spirit,
one God forever and ever.

Personal Conversation with Jesus

- What is a new way you feel called to serve?

- Thank God for your specific vocation.

- Pray for young men and women in your parish to discern a call to priesthood and religious life.

Dismissal

At one time the Mass's dismissal words were Ite, missa est, *meaning "Go, you are sent." Remember, the liturgy does not simply come to an end. Nowadays the priest or deacon may say one of the following dismissal statements. For each we respond, "Thanks be to God."*

> Go forth, the Mass is ended.
> Go and announce the Gospel of the Lord.
> Go in peace, glorifying the Lord by your life.
> Go in peace.

Personal Conversation with Jesus

- Concretely apply the meaning of each statement to your life.

- What is a one-sentence announcement of the Gospel of the Lord that you wish to share?

- Pray for peace.

Veni, Creator Spiritus

This traditional ninth-century prayer is an invocation to the Holy Spirit. Translated, Veni, Creator Spiritus means "Come, Creator Spirit." The prayer is often used in liturgical celebrations, including the Feast of Pentecost. It is also widely prayed in the Anglican Church. Martin Luther wrote a paraphrased version of the prayer in German. We ask the Paraclete to guide us and protect us from evil.

Come, Holy Spirit, Creator blest,

and in our souls take up Thy rest;
come with Thy grace and heavenly aid
to fill the hearts which Thou hast made.

O comforter, to Thee we cry,
O heavenly gift of God Most High,
O fount of life and fire of love,
and sweet anointing from above.

Thou in Thy sevenfold gifts are known;
Thou, finger of God's hand we own;
Thou, promise of the Father, Thou
Who dost the tongue with power imbue.

Kindle our sense from above,
and make our hearts o'erflow with love;
with patience firm and virtue high
the weakness of our flesh supply.

Far from us drive the foe we dread,
and grant us Thy peace instead;
so shall we not, with Thee for guide,
turn from the path of life aside.

Oh, may Thy grace on us bestow
the Father and the Son to know;
and Thee, through endless times
    confessed,
of both the eternal Spirit blest.

Now to the Father and the Son,
Who rose from death, be glory given,
with Thou, O Holy Comforter,
henceforth by all in earth and heaven.
Amen.

Personal Conversation with Jesus

- Pray "Come, Holy Spirit" as a mantra.

- Imagine your heart overflowing for love in new ways. What will those ways look like?

- Ask Jesus through the Holy Spirit to drive all evil from your life.

The Benedictus

The Benedictus originates from the song of thanksgiving given by Zechariah at the birth of his son, John the Baptist. It is recorded in Luke 1:68–79. The canticle is divided into two parts. The first part (verses 68–75) is a song of thanksgiving for God's answering the prayers for a Messiah. The second part (verses 76–79) is Zachary's words to his son, who was to be the prophet who would preach the remission of sins before the coming of Jesus. In Zechariah's address to John the Baptist, we likewise find our direction to "prepare the way of the Lord" in all that we do and say.

Blessed be the Lord, the God of Israel,
    for he has visited and brought redemption
        to his people.
He has raised up a horn for our salvation
    within the house of David his servant,
even as he promised through the mouth of his
    holy prophets from of old:
    salvation from our enemies and from the
        hand of all who hate us,
to show mercy to our fathers
    and to be mindful of his holy covenant
and of the oath he swore to Abraham our
    father,
    and to grant us that, rescued from the hand
        of enemies,

without fear we might worship him in holiness
and righteousness
before him all our days.
And you, child, will be called prophet of the
Most High,
for you will go before the Lord to prepare
his ways,
to give his people knowledge of salvation
through the forgiveness of their sins,
because of the tender mercy of our God
by which the daybreak from on high will
visit us
to shine on those who sit in darkness and death's
shadow,
to guide our feet into the path of peace.

Personal Conversation with Jesus

- How is Jesus your Savior?

- Ask Jesus for his help in proclaiming to all the
knowledge of salvation.

- Pray "*Maranatha*" ("Come, Lord Jesus") in anticipa-
tion of the Lord's Second Coming.

Deuteronomy 10:12-13, 20-21

The Old Testament warns against serving false gods and encourages instead paying all allegiance to the one, true God who is Creator of all. Although the Old Testament is made up of laws that direct the most minute of behaviors, the heart of the Law is to love and serve God with resoluteness.

Now, therefore, Israel, what does the LORD, your God, ask of you but to fear the LORD, your God, to follow in all his ways, to love and serve the LORD, your God, with your whole heart and with your whole being, to keep the commandments and statutes of the LORD that I am commanding you today for your own well-being? . . .

The LORD, your God, shall you fear, and him shall you serve; to him hold fast and by his name shall you swear. He is your praise; he is your God, who has done for you those great and awesome things that your own eyes have seen.

Personal Conversation with Jesus

- To fear the Lord is to be in awe of his majesty. Thank the eternal God for being a loving God.

- What are the "ways" of the Lord that you must follow?

- Praise Jesus. Promise you will serve him.

Psalm 96:1-6, 9b-10a

All of humanity is invited to praise the glory of God. We are to proclaim his greatness by our own lives and declare his sovereignty over all.

Sing to the LORD a new song;
> sing to the LORD, all the earth.

Sing to the LORD, bless his name;
> proclaim his salvation day after day.

Tell his glory among the nations;
> among all peoples, his marvelous deeds.

For great is the LORD and highly to be praised,
> to be feared above all gods.

For the gods of the nations are idols,
> but the LORD made the heavens.

Splendor and power go before him;
> power and grandeur are in his holy place.

. . .

Tremble before him, all the earth;
> declare among the nations: The LORD is
> king.

Personal Conversation with Jesus

- Share a new song of praise to the Lord from the deepest part of your being.

- Quietly sing a favorite liturgical hymn of praise.

- Dismiss the false gods in your life.

Acts 1:6-9

Even after his Resurrection, the disciples misunderstood Jesus to be a political leader who would establish an earthly kingdom. Jesus's kingdom is not of this earth, however, and it was the disciples' given task to share this news from Jerusalem, the city where salvation was accomplished, to the ends of the earth. The same task belongs to us as modern-day disciples.

> When they had gathered together they asked him, "Lord, are you going to restore the kingdom to Israel?" He answered them, "It is not for you to know the times or seasons that the Father has established by his own authority. But you will receive power when the holy Spirit comes upon you, and you will be my witnesses in Jerusalem, throughout Judea and Samaria, and to the ends of the earth." When he had said this, as they were looking on, he was lifted up, and a cloud took him from their sight.

Personal Conversation with Jesus

- Ask Jesus to clarify your mission as his disciple.

- Who is someone you know who needs to hear the Good News? How might you share it with this person?

- Tell Jesus how much you desire his Second Coming.

Mark 10:42-45

Our status and esteem in life is based only in our service to God and others. Jesus's service is his Passion and Death for the forgiveness of sins of the human race. The greatest action of a disciple is to be a servant of all. The dismissal at Mass is a reminder to begin this mission as soon as we exit the church doors.

Jesus summoned them and said to them, "You know that those who are recognized as rulers over the Gentiles lord it over them, and their great ones make their authority over them felt. But it shall not be so among you. Rather, whoever wishes to be great among you will be your servant; whoever wishes to be first among you will be the slave of all. For the Son of Man did not come to be served but to serve and to give his life as ransom for many."

Personal Conversation with Jesus

- Ponder Jesus's style of servant leadership.

- Whom are you called to serve?

- Are you willing to give up your life for Jesus? Pray over your answer to this question with Jesus.

Venerable Archbishop Fulton J. Sheen: We Identify with Those in Need

Archbishop Fulton J. Sheen, known for his preaching on television in the 1950s and beyond, once described our participation in the Eucharist in three "acts." In the first act, we offer ourselves to Christ; in the second act, we die with him; and in the third act, we receive new life: "No one ever dies with Christ without receiving new life. Now that we have died to that which is lower, we have the higher life," Archbishop Sheen said. With our new life in Christ, we must also identify with those most in need, he explained further.

> So long as there are poor,
> I am poor.
> So long as there are prisons,
> I am a prisoner.
> So long as there are sick,
> I am weak.
> So long as there is ignorance,
> I must learn the truth.
> So long as there is hate,
> I must love.
> So long as there is hunger,
> I am famished.

Such is the identification Our Divine
Lord would have us make with all whom
He made in love and for love.

Personal Conversation with Jesus

- Ask Jesus: "How can I love more?"

- Pray for those identified: the poor, prisoners, the
  sick, the ignorant, the hated, and the hungry.

- Think about someone despised in society or by you
  personally. Remember this person is created in love
  by the God who created you.

Servant of God Dorothy Day: We Are All One

Dorothy Day, a Catholic social activist of the twentieth century, preached nonviolence and pacifism as the core of social change. She spoke out against every war of the twentieth century. She was the founder of the Catholic Worker Movement and the newspaper that goes by that name. Dorothy Day believed that by making ourselves poor, "we increase our knowledge of and belief in love." On the same topic, she added the following:

We cannot love God unless we love each other, and to love we must know each other. We know Him in the breaking of bread, and we know each other in the breaking of bread, and we are not alone anymore. Heaven is a banquet and life is a banquet, too, even with a crust, where there is companionship.

True love is delicate and kind, full of gentle perception and understanding, full of beauty and grace, full of joy unutterable.

There should be some flavor of this in all our love for others. We are all one. We are one flesh in the Mystical Body as man and woman are said to be one flesh in marriage. With such a love one would see all things new; we would begin to see people as they really are, as God sees them.

Personal Conversation with Jesus

- Meditate on the heavenly banquet. Who is there with you? What is it like?

- Imagine the human family—past, present, and future—as one flesh in the Mystical Body of Jesus.

- How does God see you? Think honestly and deeply on this question.

Pope Francis: It Is God Who Serves Us

As part of a Holy Thursday address in 2020 during the COVID-19 pandemic, Pope Francis spoke of how our own service of neighbor must only be viewed in the loving way that God has first served us.

God saved us by serving us. We often think we are the ones who serve God. No, he is the one who freely chose to serve us, for he loved us first. It is difficult to love and not be loved in return. And it is even more difficult to serve if we do not let ourselves be served by God. . . .

We can think of all the small or great betrayals that we have suffered in life. It is terrible to discover that a firmly placed trust has been betrayed. From deep within our heart a disappointment surges up that can even make life seem meaningless. This happens because we were born to be loved and to love, and the most painful thing is to be betrayed by someone who promised to be loyal and close to us. We cannot even imagine

how painful it was for God who is love.
. . .

How many falsehoods, hypocrisies and duplicities! How many good intentions betrayed! How many broken promises! How many resolutions left unfulfilled! The Lord knows our hearts better than we do. He knows how weak and irresolute we are, how many times we fall, how hard it is for us to get up and how difficult it is to heal certain wounds. And what did he do in order to come to our aid and serve us? He told us through the Prophet: "I will heal their faithlessness; I will love them deeply" (*Hos* 14:5). . . .

That is the extent to which Jesus served us: he descended into the abyss of our most bitter sufferings, culminating in betrayal and abandonment. Today, in the face of the many false securities that have now crumbled, in the face of so many hopes betrayed, in the sense of abandonment that weighs upon our hearts, Jesus says to each one of us: "Courage, open your heart to my love. You will feel the consolation of God who sustains you." . . .

We were put in this world to love him and our neighbors. Everything else passes away, only this remains. The tragedy we are experiencing at this time summons us to take seriously the things that are serious, and not to be caught up in those that matter less; to rediscover that life is of no use if not used to serve others. For life is measured by love.

Personal Conversation with Jesus

- Tell Jesus about a time when you were betrayed by another. Tell him how the experience made you feel.

- Describe the courage it takes to open yourself to love after a betrayal.

- How does serving another benefit you?

St. John Henry Newman: We Are All One

St. John Henry Newman, canonized by Pope Francis in 2019, is the author of many classic books on the faith. Before leaving the Anglican Church to become Catholic in the mid-nineteenth century, he wrote Essay on the Development of Christian Doctrine, *a seminal piece in which he withdrew his former negative critique of Roman Catholicism. In the following short meditation sometimes titled "The Mission of My Life," St. John Henry Newman offers direction for anyone trying to discern their life's calling.*

God has created me to do Him some definite service. He has committed some work to me which He has not committed to another. I have my mission. I may never know it in this life, but I shall be told it in the next. I am a link in a chain, a bond of connection between persons. He has not created me for naught. I shall do good; I shall do His work. I shall be an angel of peace, a preacher of truth in my own place, while not intending it if I do but keep His commandments. Therefore, I will trust Him, whatever I am, I can never be thrown away. If I am in sickness, my sickness may serve Him, in perplexity, my perplexity may serve Him. If I am in sorrow, my sorrow may serve Him. He does nothing in vain. He knows what He is about. He may take away my friends. He may throw me among strangers. He may make me feel desolate, make my spirits sink, hide my future from me. Still, He knows what He is about.

Personal Conversation with Jesus

- Pray with Jesus about what he has called you to do in your life.
- Recommit yourself to trusting the Lord.
- How can you serve God this very day?

Redemptionis Donum:
"You Will Have Treasure in Heaven"

Redemptionis Donum *(The Gift of the Redemption) is a 1984 apostolic exhortation by St. John Paul II on consecrated life. In the following message (no. 5), he offers words about the call that is common to our baptismal vocation to lose our lives for the Gospel.*

Vocation carries with it the answer to the question: Why be a human person—and how? This answer adds a new dimension to the whole of life and establishes its definitive meaning. This meaning emerges against the background of the Gospel paradox of losing one's life in order to save it, and on the other hand saving one's life by losing it "for Christ's sake and for the sake of the Gospel," as we read in Mark.

In the light of these words, Christ's call becomes perfectly clear: "Go, sell what you possess, and give to the poor, and you will have treasure in heaven; and come, follow me." Between this "go" and the subsequent "come, follow me" there is a close connection. It can be said that these latter words determine the very essence of vocation. For a vocation is a matter of following the footsteps of Christ (*sequi*—to follow, hence *sequela Christi*). The terms "go . . . sell . . . give" seem to lay down the precondition of a vocation. Nevertheless, this condition is not "external" to a vocation but is already inside it. For a person discovers the new sense of his or her humanity not only in order "to follow" Christ but to the extent that he or she actually does follow Him. When a person "sells what he possesses" and "gives it to the poor," he discovers that those possessions and the comforts he enjoyed were not the treasure to hold on to. The treasure is in his heart, which Christ makes capable of "giving" to others by the giving of self. The rich person is not the one who possesses but the one who "gives," the one who is capable of giving.

Personal Conversation with Jesus

- How are you rich when you give away your possessions?

- Ask Jesus to tell you what he wishes for you to give up in order to follow him.

- Pray to be capable of giving to others.

Catechism of the Catholic Church:
Rising to Divine Love

St. Paul defined the qualities of true charity in the First Letter to the Corinthians (13:4–7). Christian charity is the practice of all the virtues that are governed by love (see Catechism of the Catholic Church, *1825, 1827, below). Christian love is supernatural; it enables us to live beyond the powers of our human nature and offers the opportunity to rise to the perfection of divine love.*

Christ died out of love for us, while we were still "enemies." The Lord asks us to love as he does, even our *enemies*, to make ourselves the neighbor of those farthest away, and to love children and the poor as Christ himself. . . .

The practice of all the virtues is animated and inspired by charity, which "binds everything together in perfect harmony"; it is the *form of the virtues*; it articulates and orders them among themselves; it is the source and the goal of their Christian practice. Charity upholds and purifies our human ability to love, and raises it to the supernatural perfection of divine love.

Personal Conversation with Jesus

- Pray for an "enemy."

- Repeat the mantra "Help me love as you love, Jesus."

- Reflect on divine love, which has no beginning or end.

Laudato si': Beyond the Sun

Laudato si' *(*Praise Be to You*) with the subtitle "On Care for Our Common Home" is Pope Francis's 2015 encyclical that laments human carelessness toward our environment and encourages us to make personal and societal changes to better care for our planet. In the concluding paragraphs (243–45), he reminds us that in eternal life "beyond the sun" we will experience infinite beauty, but for now we must be concerned with protecting our common earthly home.*

> At the end, we will find ourselves face to face with the infinite beauty of God (cf. 1 Cor 13:12), and be able to read with admiration and happiness the mystery of the universe, which with us will share in unending plenitude. Even now we are journeying towards the sabbath of eternity, the new Jerusalem, towards our common home in heaven. Jesus says: "I make all things new" (Rev 21:5). Eternal life will be a shared experience of awe, in which each creature, resplendently transfigured, will take its rightful place and have something to give those poor men and women who will have been liberated once and for all.

In the meantime, we come together to take charge of this home which has been entrusted to us, knowing that all the good which exists here will be taken up into the heavenly feast. In union with all creatures, we journey through this land seeking God, for "if the world has a beginning and if it has been created, we must enquire who gave it this beginning, and who was its Creator." Let us sing as we go. May our struggles and our concern for this planet never take away the joy of our hope.

God, who calls us to generous commitment and to give him our all, offers us the light and the strength needed to continue on our way. In the heart of this world, the Lord of life, who loves us so much, is always present. He does not abandon us, he does not leave us alone, for he has united himself definitively to our earth, and his love constantly impels us to find new ways forward. *Praise be to him*!

Personal Conversation with Jesus

- Formulate a plan to help care for the planet.

- Pray this mantra: "Make all things new, Jesus."

- Imagine those who are poor, disabled, and lonely in positions of honor in the eternal kingdom.

The Nicene Creed: What We Believe

The First Council of Nicaea was called in AD 325 by the emperor Constantine in conjunction with Pope Sylvester I's response to Arianism, a heretical belief named for an Alexandrian priest that denied Jesus's divinity by claiming that Jesus was not of the same substance as God the Father. The Council condemned Arianism and approved a creed that spelled out that Jesus is consubstantial or "of the same substance" with the Father. It also affirmed that Christ was "true God from true God, begotten not made." These two affirmations opened the door for a more substantial understanding of the Blessed Trinity. The Nicene Creed, proclaiming Jesus's divinity and equality to the Father, is recited by Catholics at Mass to this day.

I believe in one God,
the Father almighty,
maker of heaven and earth,
of all things visible and invisible.

I believe in one Lord Jesus Christ,
the Only Begotten Son of God,
born of the Father before all ages.

God from God, Light from Light,
true God from true God,

begotten, not made, consubstantial with
  the Father;
through him all things were made.

For us men and for our salvation
he came down from heaven,
and by the Holy Spirit was incarnate of
the Virgin Mary,
and became man.

For our sake he was crucified under
Pontius Pilate,
he suffered death and was buried,
and rose again on the third day
in accordance with the Scriptures.

He ascended into heaven
and is seated at the right hand of the
Father.
He will come again in glory
to judge the living and the dead
and his kingdom will have no end.

I believe in the Holy Spirit, the Lord,
the giver of life,
who proceeds from the Father and the
Son,

who with the Father and the Son is
adored and glorified,
who has spoken through the prophets.

I believe in one, holy, catholic and apostolic Church.
I confess one Baptism for the forgiveness of sins
and I look forward to the resurrection of the dead
and the life of the world to come. Amen.

Personal Conversation with Jesus

- Ask Jesus to shed light on each of these creedal statements.

- Meditate on and affirm your belief in these creedal statements.

- Pray to the Blessed Trinity.

Appendix
Additional Resources for Adoration

Listed in this section are additional materials and references for Eucharistic Adoration.

Prayers and Devotions

Prayer before Meditation by St. John Henry Newman

I place myself in the presence of Him, in whose Incarnate Presence I am before. I place myself there.

I adore Thee, O my Savior, present here as God and man, in soul and body, in true flesh and blood.

I acknowledge and confess that I kneel before that Sacred Humanity, which was conceived in Mary's womb and lay in Mary's bosom; which grew up to man's estate, and by the Sea of Galilee called the

Twelve, wrought miracles, and spoke words of wisdom and peace; which in due season hung on the cross, lay in the tomb, rose from the dead, and now reigns in heaven.

I praise, and bless, and give myself wholly to Him, Who is the true Bread of my soul, and my everlasting joy.

Act of Spiritual Communion

My Jesus, I believe that You are in the Blessed Sacrament. I love You above all things, and I long for You in my soul. Since I cannot now receive You sacramentally, come at least spiritually into my heart. As though You have already come, I embrace You and united myself entirely to You; never permit me to be separated from You.

Chaplet of Divine Mercy

Pray using Rosary beads. Begin with the Sign of the Cross and the opening prayer found on page 3.

On the first three beads say:

1 Our Father

1 Hail Mary

1 Apostles' Creed

Eternal Father, we offer you the Body and Blood, soul and divinity, of your dearly beloved Son, our Lord Jesus Christ, in atonement for our sins and those of the whole world.

On the small beads say:

V: For the sake of his sorrowful Passion,

R: have mercy on us and on the whole world.

After five decades say three times:

Holy God, Holy Mighty One, Holy Immortal One, have mercy on us and on the whole world.

Fifth Luminous Mystery of the Holy Rosary: The Institution of the Eucharist

Pray using Rosary beads. Begin with the Sign of the Cross and the Apostles' Creed.

On the first large beads say:

1 Our Father

On each of the three small beads say:

1 Hail Mary

On the second large bead say:

1 Our Father

Meditate and say a Hail Mary for each passage.

- [Jesus said to them,] "I am the bread of life. Your ancestors ate the manna in the desert, but they died; this is the bread that comes down from heaven so that one may eat it and not die." (Jn 6:48–50)

- "I am the living bread that came down from heaven; whoever eats this bread will live forever; and the bread that I will give is my flesh for the life of the world." (Jn 6:51)

- Now the Passover of the Jews was near, and many went up from the country to Jerusalem before Passover to purify themselves. They looked for Jesus and said to one another as they were in the temple area, "What do you think? That he will not come to the feast?" (Jn 11:55–56)

- On the first day of the Feast of Unleavened Bread, the disciples approached Jesus and said, "Where do you want us to prepare for you to eat the Passover?" (Mt 26:17)

- He said, "Go into the city to a certain man and tell him, 'The teacher says, "My appointed time draws near; in your house I shall celebrate the Passover with my disciples."'" (Mt 26:18)

- The disciples then did as Jesus had ordered, and prepared the Passover. (Mt 26:19)

- When it was evening, he came with the Twelve. . . . While they were eating, he took bread, said the blessing, broke it, and gave it to them and said, "Take it; this is my body." (Mk 14:17, 22)

- Then he took a cup, gave thanks, and gave it to them, and they all drank from it. He said to them, "This is my blood of the covenant, which will be shed for many." (Mk 14:23–24)

- "I tell you, from now on I shall not drink this fruit of the vine until the day when I drink it with you new in the kingdom of my Father." (Mt 26:29)

- Then, after singing a hymn, they went out to the Mount of Olives. (Mt 26:30)

Conclude by praying a Glory Be and the Fatima Prayer.
The Ave Guide to the Scriptural Rosary *(www.avemariapress. com) includes scriptural meditations for every decade of all four mysteries of the Rosary.*

Sacred Writings and Sacred Readings

Old Testament

Genesis 14:18–20

Melchizedech brought bread and wine.

Exodus 24:3–8

This is the blood of the covenant that the Lord God made with you.

Deuteronomy 10:12–22

God has chosen you because he loves you.

1 Kings 19:8

Strengthened by the food, he walked to the mountain of the Lord.

Psalms

Psalm 23

The Lord is my shepherd; there is nothing I shall want.

Psalm 34

Taste and see the goodness of the Lord.

Psalm 78

The Lord gave them bread from heaven.

Psalm 103

The Lord's kindness is everlasting to those who fear him.

New Testament

Acts 10:34a, 37–43

They ate with him after he was raised from the dead.

Hebrews 9:11–15

The blood of Christ purifies our hearts from sin.

1 Peter 1:17–21

You have been redeemed by the blood of Christ.

Revelation 7:9–14

They have washed their robes in the blood of the Lamb.

Gospels

Mark 14:12–16, 22–26

This is my body. This is my blood.

Luke 9:11b–17

All the people ate and were satisfied.

John 6:41–51

I am the living bread from heaven.

John 15:1–8

Live in me as I live in you.

Saints and Faithful Disciples

St. Thomas Aquinas

Summa Theologiae, III, q. 73–83

St. Augustine of Hippo

Sermo 227

St. Catherine of Siena

The Dialogue of St. Catherine of Siena, "A Treatise on Prayer"

St. Thérèse of Lisieux

Story of a Soul (autobiography)

Doctrines and Teachings

Didache

"Part I: The Two Ways," 1–16

The Council of Trent

Thirteenth Session

Sacrosanctum Concilium

"Chapter 2: The Most Sacred Mystery of the Eucharist"

Ecclesia de Eucharistia

Entire encyclical by St. John Paul II

ALSO AVAILABLE

The Ave Guide to the Scriptural Rosary

The Ave Guide to the Scriptural Rosary
is an attractively designed resource that will help
you pray the devotion more deeply by including
short scripture passages to read in each decade.
This hardcover keepsake includes
all of the directions, prayers, and Bible verses
you need to understand and pray a scriptural Rosary
for each of the four mysteries—Joyful, Luminous,
Sorrowful, and Glorious. Gorgeous artwork
illustrates the scripture behind each mystery.

The book also includes background on the Rosary
and its spiritual graces, how to pray
with the sacramental, and how to use
a scriptural version of the prayer.
An appendix includes Marian prayers,
a litany, a novena, and information
about Marian consecration.